ONE SECOND TO GLORY

The Alaska Adventures of Iditarod Champion Dick Mackey

OTHER BOOKS FROM
LEW FREEDMAN INCLUDE:

ACCIDENTAL ADVENTURER:
Memoirs of the First Woman to Climb Mt. McKinley,
as told to Lew Freedman

EXPLORING THE UNKNOWN:
Historic Diaries of Bradford Washburn's Alaska/Yukon
Expeditions, edited by Lew Freedman

FATHER OF THE IDITAROD:
The Joe Redington Story

IDITAROD CLASSICS:
Tales of the Trail told by the Men and Women
Who Race Across Alaska

IDITAROD DREAMS:
A Year in the Life of Iditarod driver DeeDee Jenrowe

IDITAROD SILVER

SPIRIT OF THE WIND:
The Story of Alaska's George Attla, Legendary
Sled Dog Sprint Champ

ONE SECOND TO GLORY

The Alaska Adventures of Iditarod Champion Dick Mackey

Memoir
As told to Lew Freedman

EPICENTER PRESS

Alaska Book Adventures

Epicenter Press is a regional press founded in Alaska whose interests include but are not limited to the arts, history, nature, and diverse cultures and lifestyles of the North Pacific and high latitudes. Epicenter seeks both the traditional and innovative in publishing high-quality nonfiction books and contemporary art and photography gift books.

Publisher: Kent Sturgis
Cover Design: Elizabeth Watson, Watson Design
Text design: Victoria Sturgis
Proofreader: Sherrill Carlson
Map: Marge Muehler, Gray Mouse Graphics
Printer: CDS Documentation

Library of Congress Control Number: 2001094970
ISBN 0-9708493-4-6

To order extra copies of ONE SECOND TO GLORY, mail $16.95 plus $4.95 to Epicenter Press, Box 82368, Kenmore, WA 98028. WA residents add $1.50 for state sales tax. You also may order via fax to (425) 481-8253, via phone to (800) 950-6663, or at our website, EpicenterPress.com.

Booksellers: Retail discounts are available from our trade distributor, Graphic Arts Center Publishing™, Box 10306, Portland, OR 97210.

First Edition
First printing October 2001

10 9 8 7 6 5 4 3 2 1

In loving memory of my parents, Eno
and Shirley Mackey, for making me as I am.
And to my family, each of whom in their own way
has contributed to the fulfillment of my life.

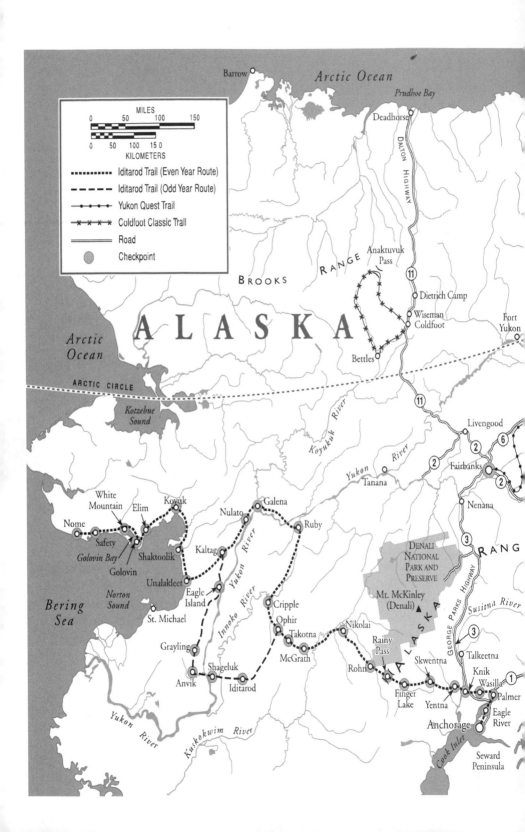

TABLE OF CONTENTS

INTRODUCTION

A road stop enroute to Coldfoot with Lew Freedman in August 2000.
Lew Freedman

NORTH. As far as you can drive. In August 2000 Dick Mackey and I were driving the Dalton Highway, Alaska's infamous Haul Road. Built in the 1970s as a transportation route to carry supplies for the construction of the 800-mile trans-Alaska Pipeline, the Dalton Highway is a mostly dirt and gravel road that forms the spine of the state.

We were on our way to Coldfoot, the farthest-north public truck stop in the world, above the Arctic Circle, on the road to the Prudhoe Bay oil fields. Coldfoot is aptly named because the lowest-ever temperature in North America was recorded there. It is a blip on the map. In a vast region with more caribou than people, crossed by more tractor-trailers than automobiles, Coldfoot is a way station. It is an oasis in the Brooks Range, a mountainous haven for lonely truckers seeking a hot cup of coffee and warm conversation on the long drive to and from the oilfields on the northern coast.

Lately, Coldfoot has come into its own as a destination for adventurous souls who wish to see unspoiled, remote Alaska, and don't mind driving a couple of hundred miles over a rough road to do it.

Dick Mackey *made* Coldfoot. Already famous throughout Alaska for a mushing career that spanned the glory years of the Anchorage Fur Rendezvous World Championship Sled Dog Race and the early days of the Iditarod Trail Sled Dog Race, which he won in 1978 by one second, Mackey transformed a wilderness outpost into the world's farthest-north public truck stop and an offbeat, quirky destination.

Mackey likes to say that mushing was his first love, but his true purpose for coming to Alaska from New Hampshire was to found Coldfoot.

"In the early 1980s," he said, "it was still somewhat of a daring adventure to come up here."

And it still can be, what with a few hundred miles of hazardous road and a couple of hundred days a year sure to bring hazardous weather.

Mackey's Alaska adventures span virtually the whole state. He was the man who built Coldfoot from nothing into something unique. He was an ironworker who helped raise the most important buildings in several communities. He was a hunter feeding his family. He was a pilot who flew his bush plane all over the state's 586,000 square miles. He worked for the Alaska Railroad. And he was a commercial fish processor and fish buyer.

Between the 1950s and the turn of the new century, he was a first-hand witness to monumental change. When he arrived, 45,000 people lived in Anchorage, Alaska's largest city. Now there are 260,000.

"I used to hunt rabbits where the Northway Mall is today," he likes to say of one of the state's largest shopping centers.

Mackey was a dog musher whose legacy includes helping to establish the Iditarod, the world-famous eleven-hundred mile race that passes through Alaska's wild Interior from Anchorage to Nome. He also sired a mushing family that produced Rick Mackey, the 1983 Iditarod champ. Dick and Rick are the only father-son title-holders in the event that got its start in 1973.

Rick Mackey says mushing was the family activity when he was a kid.

"That's just what we did every weekend," he said.

And dad was the main influence, loading the kids into the truck and driving all over Southcentral Alaska for races.

Rick Mackey remembers the joy when his father won the Iditarod. "That was a great day," he said.

Being not only the first, but also the only father-son combination to capture Iditarod titles, is gratifying and a distinction appreciated by the family.

"It means a lot," said Rick Mackey. "It's been special over the years, and it still is."

The drama surrounding Dick Mackey's momentous Iditarod victory, besting defending champion and Iditarod legend Rick Swenson, endures in mushing history. Who could ever imagine a photo finish in a 1,100-mile sled dog race?

Perhaps only Alaskan residents can appreciate the esteem in which Iditarod champions are held. In a state with no major professional sports teams, Iditarod champions are the superstar athletes. In a state with a healthy respect for winter, Iditarod champions are the hardiest of the hardy, emblematic of a throwback era.

Some of those champions are more revered or better known than others. Years after his famous finish, Mackey has not faded into the woodwork. Although retired from mushing, he has remained in the public eye. He served as television commentator for Alaska mushing events; the race director of a sled-dog race in Italy; race marshal of the Iron Dog, the world's longest snowmachine race; and on the board of directors of the Yukon Quest, a 1,000-mile international sled dog race between Fairbanks, Alaska, and Whitehorse, Yukon Territory. Mackey played tour guide for well-to-do tourists driving their own recreational vehicles to Alaska. He was hired as a consultant for the filming of *White Fang*, the famous Jack London story from the gold-rush era.

Maybe this explains why Mackey is so well known and remembered. Still, he attributes most of his enduring notoriety to the one-second finish. Not a day goes by, he said, that someone doesn't bring it up. This claim was hard to believe, but I became a believer.

On the day we drove from Mackey's home in Nenana to Coldfoot, he mentioned how often his then twenty-two-year-old Iditarod victory is a topic of conversation. Not two hours later, standing at the cash register in the restaurant at Coldfoot, a man he had never seen before accosted him.

"Dick Mackey!" the man exclaimed. "I have a photograph of you at the finish line from 1978. Will you autograph it for me?"

Mackey has a distinctive, recognizable face—angular, sharp-featured, and white-haired. Mackey remains trim, seemingly capable of jumping on the back of a sled on short notice and once again mushing to Nome, even as he pushes seventy.

And Mackey has a voice familiar to Alaskans, too. He enunciates precisely and, forty-something years after departing New England, he retains an accent from the region.

Certainly truckers on the Dalton Highway caught the inflections and identified them swiftly, As we drove along, Mackey unhooked the microphone of a CB radio in his pickup truck and addressed passing truckers. It had been a decade since he operated Coldfoot, but many of the same truckers made their living hauling freight along this desolate road.

One big semi passed us, and Mackey was sure he knew the driver. When he hailed the trucker, the call came back immediately, "Hey, Dick, what are you doing?"

Yes, they still know Dick Mackey way up north near Coldfoot.

Coldfoot—and the truckers he served and befriended—remain close to Mackey's heart. He made Coldfoot much more than a fuel stop with the simple philosophy: "What the hell kind of highway have you got here if you can't get a cup of coffee?"

Coffee was indeed the staple beverage of Coldfoot, a place that could have been named "Cold" because a lot more than feet got chilled there. One winter the temperature dropped to 82 degrees below zero.

"I planned to go for three months and stayed for nine years," said Mackey.

It was somewhat of an occasion when Mackey returned to Coldfoot. Truckers repeatedly asked if he was going to take over again. The owners treated him like royalty. After working his way through the buffet line for a hearty dinner of ribs, rice, beans, fish, salad, and coffee, Mackey admired a framed photograph on the wall. The picture focuses on a trailer hitch in front of a truck, a blue bus, and a wall tent. Mackey arrived at Coldfoot on June 15, 1981. The photo was taken the next morning.

"You built that?" a woman joked, pointing to the tent.

He built *from* that.

When Dick Mackey came to Alaska in the 1950s, he was a poor man anxious to provide a better life for his family. He built from that, too.

Lew Freedman

GREAT MUSHING MOMENTS

Dick Mackey's Iditarod Career

1973—Second musher to sign up for first race
1973—Seventh place
1974—Tenth place
1975—Seventh place
1976—Eighth place
1977—Sixth place
1978—First place
1987—Thirty-second place
1988—Inducted into the Iditarod Hall of Fame

Iditarod director, 1973-86
Iditarod president, 1979
Iditarod trail manager, 1981 and 1985

TRADING CARDS

Photo finish on Front Street

*Running just ahead of me about two miles from
the finish, Rick looked back and said we had it made — him
first and me second. "Yeah, right,"I thought.*

That's me in the middle, jubilant after finishing the Iditarod in 1974.
©Richard Burmeister/Alaska Stock Images

ONE SECOND.

In 1978, I won the Iditarod Trail Sled Dog Race, one second ahead of
Rick Swenson, after a 1,100-mile race from Anchorage to Nome. They called
it a photo finish, but you could see the difference with the naked eye.

This was the crowning moment of my mushing career and the most
spectacular not to mention closest finish in Iditarod history. If you saw it, if
you were part of it, you never forgot it. The public reaction helped put the
Iditarod on the map.

What a scene it was. Rick and I came running down Front Street along side our dog teams, sweat pouring off of us, our breath forming little clouds of fog. This was the culmination of more than two weeks on the trail, the end of a race filled with gamesmanship and cooperation, hard work, and hard-driving dogs.

We were too hot. I was wearing a parka designed to keep me warm at 70 below zero but on Front Street the temperature was above zero. My bib number was tied on so tight I couldn't get my coat off. I was melting.

The word was out that the finish would be close. Thousands of fans jammed the street and sidewalks the last one-half mile. Everybody was down on Front Street and they were going ape. It was crazy.

It was so tight we could barely mush our teams through the crush of people.

Young Rick Swenson was the defending champion and favorite to win the world's longest sled-dog race again. He was nearly twenty years younger than me. I was forty-five. I had been mushing for a while and was the old-timer. Maybe I was the sentimental favorite, but I wasn't the betting favorite. Swenson went on to win five Iditarod races, more than anyone else, but I stole this one right from under his nose.

I played a lot of head games that year. Some of them were with Rick and some were through the newspapers. By the time we reached Unalakleet, with close to three hundred miles to go, we agreed not to speak to each other the rest of the trip.

That didn't last. We did speak to each other. And sometimes we got upset with each other. No doubt about it. He was more upset with me than I was with him. Coming out of Golovin, he said, "I just can't get rid of you, can I?" I just grinned. That was part of the psyche job. We still had other mushers to contend with, too. Emmitt Peters was still right in there as were the Anderson boys, Eep and Babe. Swenson and I were fourth and fifth out of White Mountain, and no way did we have the race wrapped up. But we overwhelmed them. Babe Anderson got caught in a storm, and didn't even finish.

Emmitt was still hovering, but we went by him so fast and didn't think he would be a factor. It was obvious Rick and I would be dueling it out. And we did.

Rick and I had mushed more or less together for hundreds of miles, and I knew I had the team to beat him. He was confident, even cocky, believing that he was the best. If you want to be a champion you've got to have some of that attitude. I had figured out well back on the trail that I had the dogs that could take Swenson if I positioned myself well.

However, my optimism began to fade as we neared Nome. Rick Swenson is a superb dog man. We got down to the last two miles, coming off the sea ice of Norton Sound, up over the sea wall onto the road that leads into Nome, and I wasn't sure I was going to win. Until then we'd had worried about Emmitt Peters catching us. We were looking over our shoulders.

Then Rick said that we had it made, him first and me second, and that I should just stay right behind him. I thought, "Yeah, right, we'll see how it's going to end up."

I reached into my sled bag and I pulled out a whip. And he reached into his bag and pulled out a whip too. We were like jockeys on the home stretch. Nobody uses whips in the Iditarod anymore, but in the 1970s they were common.

We passed the Fort Davis Roadhouse, first and second, him still in the lead. But my lead dog was no more than five feet behind Rick's heels as he stood on the sled runners.

We were so close together as we started down Front Street that when Rick cracked that whip in the air, unknown to him it flew back and struck right across the face of one of my lead dogs. I cussed him out. When that happened, my dogs veered over to the sidewalk toward the big, yellow state government building. I had to run to the front of the dogs and straighten them out.

Rick had his own problems. "Blueberry" John, who drove summer tour buses, had one of his old school buses parked along the street, and Swenson's team got hung up on the bus. While I was untangling my team from the spectators, he was trying to detach his team from the bus. I doubt either of us was thinking about winning at that moment so much as just making it to the finish line through the people.

In today's Iditarod, the finish line is set apart from the crowd and from motor traffic by a chute of hurricane fencing. But in the early days, the finish line angled back right up to the sidewalk. The street was completely shut down. People were everywhere.

So here we came huffing up the street. The dogs were moving again, and I was running alongside them. Sweat ran off me like water, and I couldn't catch my breath. Then there was one more problem. A German film crew had set up on the edge of the fencing with a tripod and camera over it. My dogs ran right into the tripod and stopped. At that point I wasn't paying any attention to Swenson.

Again I ran to the front of my team and pulled away the leaders, Skipper and Shrew, then ran back to the sled and got them going again. The crowd was going bananas. The moment I saw my leaders run beneath the burled arch that marks the finish line I went limp and fell onto the sled. The only thing was, I missed the sled and fell flat onto the snow. My heart was pounding and my lungs were bursting. Somebody yelled, "Oh, God, he's had a heart attack!" It was no heart attack, but I knew I had finished and was ready for a rest.

Swenson came across. As soon as his leaders crossed the line, he stopped too. From that point on, there was confusion.

Some people were confused about who had won. Was it me because my dogs crossed the finish line first? Or was it Swenson because after stopping he moved his whole outfit across the finish line?

It was chaotic. Nobody had ever seen anything like it. The timer was Leo Rasmussen, who later became mayor of Nome and served as president of the Iditarod Trail Committee. He was down on his knees in the snow, looking between other officials' legs, and he was the one who declared that one second separated me from Swenson.

My chest was heaving, and the roar of the crowd was unbelievable. But I knew I had won. Swenson knew I had won. Every race there ever was, all you had to do was break the plane of the finish line. I could have been dragging the dogs backwards and reached out and touched the plane of the finish line, and won.

The only stipulation was that you had to be with your sled. You had to be a continuous part of the team. During the All-Alaska Sweepstakes in Nome a century ago, with rules set out by the Nome Kennel Club, the sled and musher both had to cross the line to constitute a finish. We weren't running under the old rules.

In those early years, the late Dick Tozier was the regular Iditarod race marshal. But he was ill during the 1978 race and had stayed behind in Anchorage. Bud Smyth and Myron Gavin were co-race marshals. Tom Busch, a reporter from KNOM radio, and a few others were muttering that a team, sled, and driver had to move all the way across the finish line for a finish to be official. So Swenson pushed his team across. And Tom congratulated him. Swenson said, "For what, coming in second?" And darned if Al Crane, president of the Nome Kennel Club, didn't declare Swenson the winner.

The saving grace in all this brouhaha was that I knew I won and Swenson knew I won. The officials got on the phone to Tozier and after the circumstances were explained, he asked why they were even bothering him. There was no question—I had won.

Then Myron stepped in and said that of course Mackey had won. What he said would be remembered for all time, comparing our finish to a photo finish in a horse race:

"They don't take a picture of the horse's ass, do they?"

I took home the championship trophy in 1978. How sweet it was!

What to do with my life?

I was a telegraph operator at Western Union when President Truman fired General MacArthur. Hundreds of people lined up to send telegrams of protest.

This is me—a youngster in New Hampshire, wearing my first suit.

ALASKA. Growing up in New Hampshire I read stories of the north. Jack London and others. But it was never my lifelong dream to move there.

In the early 1950s, a co-worker and I decided we were going to Alaska. But my wife got pregnant, and his wife got pregnant, and that ended the discussion.

In 1959, I was twenty-six, had a family, and I was coming off hard times. I just said, "Let's go to Alaska." And we did.

It seemed like the land of opportunity, and I felt I had used up all my opportunities in New Hampshire. I guess I'm like a lot of people who become Alaskans. I was looking for a new start. Until setting out with a car full of kids on a seventeen-day drive, almost my entire life had been centered on New England.

I was born October 2, 1932 in Concord, the state capital. I was born Richard LeBlanc, then I was adopted when I was two and one-half.

I didn't know the story for a long time. It wasn't until my mother passed away that I had access to the adoption papers. My biological mother's name was Evelyn White. White is the Americanized name for LeBlanc. My father was French-Canadian, and I suspect he never became an American citizen.

At that time, pulp mills in New Hampshire hired a lot of Canadians to cut lumber. Evelyn White was from Lebanon. Apparently I had a brother, but never met him.

My adoptive father was Eric Eno Mackey. He was Finnish, born in Gloucester, Massachusetts, the famous fishing community. The family was mostly mill workers. My mother's maiden name was Shirley Martin. My father was proud of his background. He'd be the first one to tell you that Finland was the only country to repay its World War I debts to the United States.

My father's family was devastated by the flu epidemic of 1914. He lost his mother and two sisters in one week. He finished school and when he was eighteen, he moved to Concord. That was quite the deal then, to go sixty miles from home. He went to work as a messenger at a bank and worked for decades there until he retired.

My father wanted me to go into banking. I couldn't handle that kind of work. I was restless. I had a chance to attend the University of New Hampshire on an academic scholarship with my good grades in high school, but I wasn't interested in that, either.

My childhood in New Hampshire was perfect. I was rebellious, but I lived among devout churchgoers who attended the First Congregational Church of Concord. The rules were clear. You went to Sunday school and you went to church. If you had a broken leg, they carried you there, but you went. Years later, I became a born-again Christian. I don't wear it on my sleeve, but it gives me an inner peace.

As kids we played sandlot baseball and football, but at five o'clock we always came home to listen to the Jack Armstrong radio program, followed by *Terry and the Pirates* and *Captain Midnight*. You dared not miss those serials.

I was nine when World War II started. I was listening to *The Shadow* on the radio when they broke in with the bulletin that the Japanese had bombed Pearl Harbor. I ran out to the backyard to tell my parents, even though I didn't understand the gravity of the situation. But I knew was that it was bad.

I went to work on a poultry ranch the summer I was eleven, riding my bicycle four miles each way. During the war, the hired hands were two men who were over sixty-five years old and me. We each got paid fifty cents an hour, working ten hours a day, six days a week.

With my first paycheck I stopped at Ozzy Waite's sporting goods store and bought myself an old, black lunch bucket, a single-shot .22 caliber Springfield rifle for $7.98 and a box of ammunition.

The rifle was for target practice. The bank where my father worked had a basement range, and members of the police force across the way used it. My dad was a great pistol shot. He couldn't hit anything with a rifle, but he was unbelievable with a pistol. He bought me a brick of .22 rifle bullets, and I ran through them in a week.

I never imagined that later in life I would be hunting moose for my dinner table in Alaska, but by the time I bought that rifle I already had shot my first deer. From the time I was nine I never went to the first week of school because it was deer season.

My dad was a good shot, but he was not a woodsman. I got my first outdoors training from Ned Martin, my grandfather on my mother's side. He was an engineer on the Boston & Maine Railroad until he lost his job during the Depression. I can remember the next morning him leaving the house with a double-bitted axe to chop wood. That's how he was going to make a living.

For about seven years, I was his only grandson. Later my mother's sister had two boys and a girl. Their parents were protective of them, though, and did not want them to go into the woods. My parents always said, "Go with your grandfather," and I went into the hill country of New Hampshire with him all of the time.

I have spent most of my adult life in cold Alaska places, but I learned about cold in New Hampshire. We took the train forty-five miles to Grafton because no one in our family had a car. My grandfather had a camp there, and one of the farm neighbors picked us up. We vacationed there in the summer.

My grandfather had an old maple sugar house that he moved to create his camp using a couple of yokes of oxen. When I went out there with the whole family we mostly took it easy or went berry picking. When I went with my grandfather he showed me the countryside. We took hikes. He showed me an old gristmill and told me stories about settlements that dated back before the Civil War. We went fishing for trout and perch on the rivers and lakes.

On Saturday mornings, the man who owned the general store in Grafton brought meat and poultry around in a wagon. My grandfather would cut ice off the main block and store the deliveries in the icehouse.

In March, during spring vacations, I went with him to collect maple syrup. You had a half-inch brace bit and an auger and you tapped two inches into the trees. Then you tapped in a little spout. You could drive in one spout for every foot of diameter on the tree. There was a hook on the bottom of the spout supporting a two and one-half gallon bucket. You took the drippings to the sap house to be boiled. It took thirty-two gallons of sap to make a gallon of syrup.

The lifestyle was not the same as life in the Alaska wilderness, but you needed some of the same traits of self-sufficiency to make a go of it. It was rural living.

When I was older my dad became president of the Appalachian Mountain Club. We did a lot of climbing in the White Mountains. I climbed Mount Katahdin in Maine and went up all seven trails on Mount Washington. Mount Washington is more than six thousand feet high and has the strongest winds in North America. I was about fourteen the summer I climbed all over it. I was always in good shape.

Most people assume I didn't know anything about mushing until I moved to Alaska. Not true. Making the same claim of a world championship as the Anchorage Fur Rendezvous, a world championship sled-dog race was held in Laconia, New Hampshire, too. I never went to the race. Laconia was thirty-two miles away, and we didn't have a car, but I followed it in the newspaper.

We went skiing or tobogganing or ice-skating. We used to go windsailing, or ice boating, on clear-blown lakes. It seemed like we'd go a thousand miles an hour. No brakes! And nobody ever wore a helmet or any other protection. Ice boating was a big deal. So was downhill skiing. The skis were big, wooden boards, four inches wide. I had never heard of cross-country skiing.

During World War II, I became an air-raid warden's messenger. I had a hat with a civil defense insignia on it and an armband. On blackout nights I rode around the neighborhood on my bicycle with no headlamp and reported back to the warden that so-and-so had a light showing. Boy, I was big-time.

We played cowboys and Indians when I was little, and occasionally cops and robbers. We lived in a diverse community of Czechoslovakians, Armenians, Germans, and Italians. And here we were fighting the Germans and the Italians. The boys in my age group were disappointed when the war ended before we could join the fight. But we had our own junior commando unit. We had helmets and fake wooden rifles, and we trained with them. Portsmouth Navy Yard was only thirty-five miles away. When a submarine was sunk off the coast in the Atlantic Ocean it made you aware of the war.

My parents, Eno and Shirley Mackey, and me in 1950.

I did well in cross-country in high school, but mostly I worked. I was a soda jerk at Nault's Drug Store making ice-cream sodas. I also went through the Cub Scouts, Boy Scouts, and Explorers. Good training for Alaska. In 1948, I won a merit badge contest and was New Hampshire's representative to the Fillmore Ranch in New Mexico, stopping in Chicago and St. Louis on the way. We were at the ranch for a month, living in tents, hiking and riding horses. We stopped in Washington, D.C. and New York on the way home. It was a pretty good deal for a teenager!

By my junior year in high school I was working as a messenger for Western Union making thirty-five cents an hour with an extra penny added because I furnished my own bicycle. I worked afternoons and evenings.

In 1949, on my seventeenth birthday, I bought a 1933 Plymouth Coupe for $50. It was the first car in the family. It was a piece of junk. I painted it green and it had wide white sidewalls and bright yellow wire-spoke wheels. It also had a trunk that I converted into a rumble seat. It was great for attracting girls. The car lasted a year.

I brought the car home, and dad said I had to have a license. So I went down to the state house and paid a dollar for a license. There was no formal driving training. I had to have insurance, too, and that cost $17. A year later, when I renewed the license they told me that for $2 I could get a chauffeur's license. That allowed me to drive a truck. I used that license for years. I never had any training. When I moved to Alaska I had to take a written test, but not a driving test.

It was arranged that as soon as I graduated from high school I was going to go to a Western Union training school for Teletype operators. That plan changed when the driver of a Grey Van moving line truck, a subsidiary of Greyhound buses, stopped in to send a telegram. I asked where he was going, and he said Chicago. He said he could use a swamper—someone to load and unload the furniture he carried. This sounded intriguing. He said I had the job if I could be ready to leave in thirty minutes.

I ran home, grabbed my stuff, and told my mother I was going to Chicago and that I'd call her. And then I was out the door. My folks were apprehensive but gave me quite a bit of leeway. I rode all over the United States with the trucker, Jess Honey, and I was home by Labor Day weekend.

Then I went to Western Union school for a few months. My first assignment as a Teletype operator was in St. Alban's, Vermont. I turned eighteen and registered for the draft, but when the Korean War started, lo and behold they classified telegraph operators as having essential jobs. I wasn't in the Army, but I spent a year at Otis Air Force Base in Massachusetts and at Camp Edwards on Cape Cod. I was a civilian transmitting military messages, and it was awkward because I was getting paid more than the military people.

Eventually, I ended up back in St. Alban's. That's where I was working when President Harry Truman fired General Douglas MacArthur. I was awakened in the middle of the night and told to get to the office. Hundreds of people waited in line to send telegrams of complaint to the President.

I was a Western Union telegraph operator in the 1950s.

Around this time Western Union went on strike and I was vocal against the union. After that I didn't see much of a future at Western Union, so I went to work in the machine shop of Beedy Electrical Company in Penacook, about seven miles outside of Concord.

I still had no idea what I wanted to do with myself. However, my life was about to change in big ways.

Looking north 3 to the future

The New Hampshire economy was going downhill. The bank took my home. My third child had just been born. I decided we were moving to Alaska.

I bought my first truck in 1955 and went to work.

THE CONVERSATION with that co-worker about moving to Alaska took place in 1952. Alaska was creeping back into my mind.

I was married to my first wife, Joan, by then, but when she got pregnant with Rick the idea of moving to Alaska got sidetracked. Rick was born in New Hampshire in 1953.

I had met Joan Fall while working at the electrical company. She was a local gal. Once I got married and had children I had a whole new set of obligations. I think I held five different jobs the first year I was married.

I was making ninety cents an hour. A tannery was paying ninety-five cents an hour so I moved there. It went on and on like that. I was trying to get ahead. By 1954, I had a job milking on a dairy farm. It paid $35 a week and provided a house, milk and beef, and anything raised in the garden. Firewood was included, too. That was a tremendous job.

Then I accepted a job for $300 a month running another dairy farm. That made me a $10-a-day man. State employees were getting a dollar and a dime at the time. I was all by myself, milking as many as forty head a day, working from five o'clock in the morning until seven at night. A serious musher probably would have more animals in the yard than I had cows and put in a longer day.

It wore me down, so I went back to work at the tannery. In 1955, my daughter Becky was born, and I became a truck driver. Then I bought a truck. My chauffeur's license came in handy.

I was in business for myself and had a handful of drivers and trucks on the road. I was primarily hauling poultry feed and logging. Pretty soon we were feeding two and one-half million Tyson broilers all over New Hampshire, Maine, and Vermont. I also had a service truck that went to farms carrying medicines and dairy equipment.

I built a new home in Canterbury, near Concord, and was doing well until Tyson decided to move its operations to the Carolinas.

Then I had an accident. I was a twenty-four-year-old kid driving a loaded truck that hit a car driven by a seventy-year-old town selectman. He shot across an intersection in front of me. He was driving a new Buick home from the dealer. He was confused. I had no time to brake and hit him broadside. It was a bad accident.

I ended up in the hospital, but the full extent of my injury wasn't known until later. A piece of a disk broke off and it floated around in my back. To this day it's never been repaired. My leg became paralyzed. I spent six weeks in the hospital in Manchester and months at home in a body cast.

Then things went from bad to worse in my trucking business. It wasn't that I didn't work hard. I worked myself half to death. My deals were all ten-week contracts and one by one the Tyson contracts expired and weren't renewed. I owed thousands of dollars on my equipment and when the bills came due, I couldn't pay. Bankruptcy followed.

My business had fallen apart. I was in agony from my injury. By the spring of 1959, the economy in New Hampshire was going downhill. The bank took my house back. My belongings were auctioned off. And my third child, Bill, had just been born.

During this ordeal I decided we were moving to Alaska. I knew almost nothing about the new state, but it was as far away as I could drive. Somebody from my hometown had just come back from Alaska. He said, "You won't believe it—gravediggers are getting $2 an hour!" That was about double the pay for New Hampshire state jobs. I was fed up with my part of the country, fed up with everything.

I wrote communities in Alaska for information about jobs. I wrote to Anchorage. I wrote to Fairbanks. I wrote to every place I could find on the map. And I got three answers back. The letter from Juneau said, "Don't come. No work." The letter from Anchorage said, "Definitely don't come. No work." I forget where the third one was from. Some Podunk place that didn't even have a Chamber of Commerce. I decided Anchorage must be where the work was because they didn't want you there!

Morris and Betty Kelley and their three kids joined up with us. He had driven for me. I scraped together $50 through a Grange auction and bought a 1949 Chevrolet. I had my cast sawed off. I packed up my wife, three kids, and a little two-wheel trailer. That's all we had. The next day we left for Alaska.

We didn't have enough money for the trip. The Canadian government had a rule that you needed to carry cash—$300 for the driver and car and $100 for each passenger—as a condition for entering the country. It was similar to the Mounties guarding the top of the Chilkoot Pass during gold-rush days. To cross the border from Montana or Washington you needed money, and I had only $358 when I left Canterbury.

When I was younger we used to go to Montreal to party on the weekends. I figured we'd just make like we were going to Montreal for a couple of days, then drive across the country on what later was called the Trans-Canada Highway. However, when we got to the Sault Ste. Marie area of Michigan, we had to return to the States. The map was poor and so was my preparation. So we had to re-enter Canada, and didn't have enough cash.

The Canadians offered a compromise. We could buy a bond for $10. It simply guaranteed that if I broke down, or could no longer go on for any reason, the insurance policy would cover the cost of getting us to the nearest border. They just wanted to make sure we did not stay in Canada.

The second time we crossed into Canada was at Sweetgrass, Montana. Along the way we got kicked out of several places because the local people didn't allow "gypsies" in their towns. We did not look terribly flush. Bill was just a baby and disposable diapers hadn't been invented. We washed our clothes and the diapers in a stream on a rock. Then we tied the diapers onto the car door handles and dried them in the wind as we drove.

Morris had never been anywhere. I was the big-time traveler because I'd been all over the country. We got to Chicago, and Morris asked, "How much farther is it?" I laughed.

When we crossed the border from Montana, he said, "Boy, we're almost there." I didn't think so. When we got to Dawson Creek in British Columbia, he'd had it. He said he was turning around—"I won't go any farther." It did feel like we were at the end of the world.

We stopped at a little campground. We talked and talked, and finally I persuaded him to continue. I had two good arguments: first, it wasn't as far going forward as it was turning back and, second, we would find good jobs once we arrived in Alaska. That was optimistic of me. I had no idea of what lay ahead.

Until then we had been on good roads, too. Our mental picture of the Alaska Highway was of a backcountry road in New Hampshire where you hauled wood or something like that. The Alaska Highway wasn't paved then. It was a gravel road built by the military during World War II. It was still a rough road in 1959. I had seven tires that I paid almost nothing for and I blew them all.

We're talking *rough* gravel. I have pictures of being pulled through mud holes by Caterpillar tractors. When we reached the Peace River Bridge in British Columbia, we found the bridge had given way. Traffic was detoured across a wooden railroad trestle. Once we got across that I wouldn't have turned back for anything.

We were excited when we reached Whitehorse, Yukon Territory, a town of log construction. It was a metropolis compared to the roadside settlements we had driven through. Whitehorse was a welcome intermission before we got back on unpaved roads for another seven hundred fifty miles.

Even today, driving the Alaska Highway can be an adventure. Back in 1959, it was a major challenge. From the start, we knew $358 wouldn't get us to Alaska, but the way we ran through the money was another thing.

Despite the insurance of seven extra tires, I had blown them all by Kluane Lake in the Yukon Territory. There was a little Texaco Station there where I paid $28 for a brand-new tire. I was all out of spares. We had nine flat tires on the way to Alaska.

Between Fort Nelson and Summit Lodge in British Columbia the transmission had gone bad. Morris drove me to a garage. Out back was a wrecked 1947 Oldsmobile. They sold me the transmission for $50 with the idea it *might* fit into my 1949 Chevy, but with no assurance it would work. It worked, sort of. In old cars the first and reverse gears were on the same shaft. This "new" transmission didn't have any third gear. It was broken off. So we all went slower. Believe it or not when we got to Alaska I rebuilt that transmission and drove that ancient car for quite some time.

It took seventeen days to drive from New Hampshire to Anchorage. In those days you drove into Anchorage through Fort Richardson. We found ourselves in what turned out to be Mountain View. We thought this was downtown Anchorage, so we stopped there.

It was the Friday before Labor Day. I drove up and down looking around, and we ended up at Chitty's Motel. It was still there until a few years ago. Now it's a car wash. I had $14 left and we paid $7 for a room with a kitchenette for one night. So did Morris. The next morning we went to the Piggly Wiggly store and bought $7 worth of groceries.

That was my first day in Alaska. We were flat broke, we had no job prospects, and we had no idea what we were going to do.

We were pulled through a mud hole on the Alaska Highway in 1959.

Working on the railroad

*I thought Alaska was the greatest thing since sliced
bread. Statehood had been approved. Everyone was
enthused about the future, and I got caught up in it too.*

The beginnings of our homestead on Montana Creek in 1960.

ONCE IN MOUNTAIN VIEW, the Mackeys and the Kelleys split up. After the one-night stand in that motel we were on our own looking for a place to live. We bumped into a soldier who laughed after seeing the mud-covered Chevy, and said, "Looks like you just got here."

Turns out he had just bought a house that had an efficiency apartment in the back. He offered it to us for $100 a month. I said if I had $100 I'd take it, but I didn't have the cash. He said to pay him after I started work. So we had a roof over us. The food I bought with our last $7 didn't go very far, so I went to the Salvation Army and got two huge boxes of groceries. I never forgot that help.

It was a holiday weekend, so I had to wait until Tuesday to sign up at the employment office. There I discovered why people were told not to come to Anchorage. They meant it when they said there was no work. But while I was waiting in line a guy came in and announced he needed four cement block layers. I jumped in front of him and said, "Now you need three." I had put up a basement wall in my house in New Hampshire, so I wasn't lying when I told him I had experience.

I was to report at 12:30. In the meantime, I ran around the corner to the old Anchorage Hardware Store and asked what tools I needed to do a professional job. The tools sold for $17. I told the clerk I had a job waiting for me, and he took a long look at me and gave me the tools. He said to pay when I got a paycheck. He didn't even ask me to sign anything. That was Alaska in those days. Everything was done on trust. I took those shiny new tools out into the alley and scuffed them up in the gravel.

The assignment was to lay blocks for an addition to the Anchorage Times building on Fourth Avenue. We were working high up on scaffolding, and it quickly became clear that the other workers could move much faster. They were pros. Oh, man, and I'm working hard, really sweating. But I'm not working at anywhere near the pace of the other men. One of them encouraged me, saying everyone's got to learn and that I'd be all right. And then came the boss. I said, "Well, this job didn't last too long."

I felt him watching me. After a moment, he said, "Kid, come on down here. You haven't put up many cement blocks, have you?" I told him about building the basement. He looked me over and said maybe he could use me as a general hand for a couple of weeks. I said, "Boy, that would be great. At least it'll get me on my feet."

He said he couldn't pay me block layers' wages, but he could pay me $4 an hour. He said I was to haul mud to the block layers among other things. I said, "I can't earn $4 an hour." He asked what I meant. And I said, "I can't work that hard!" When told him I was from New Hampshire, he asked what did people make there. I told him anywhere from eighty-five cents to a $1.20 an hour. He said, "You'll do."

I went home and announced to my wife, "You're not going to believe it! I'm getting $4 an hour!" It was beyond comprehension. To realize how much that was to me, remember that today, forty years later, some people are working for $6 an hour.

I became a hod carrier and at that wage I was living high on the hog, even with our high rent. The boss was great. At the end of each work day he came by with a case of beer. The job didn't last long, though, and the Monday after the last Friday shift, I started working for the Alaska Railroad.

Just a few hours into my first day at the railroad I was at the bank taking out a loan for $3,500 to buy a mobile home. I must have sold the banker with my sincerity. When I asked what the monthly payments would be, he told me not to worry about it—we'd work it out. I wrote my dad, and he couldn't believe it. "Banking is not done that way," he said. Well, banking was done that way up north at that time. Once again Alaska welcomed us.

I thought Alaska was the greatest thing since sliced bread. Statehood had been approved only a few months before. Everybody was all enthused. Everyone believed in Alaska and its future, and I was all caught up in it, too. Look what everyone was doing for me.

I worked for the railroad for five years, including regular winter layoffs. One day in the freight shed a customer urged me to homestead in Talkeetna. I was polite about how nice that would be. "I know where there's some land," he said.

He came back a week or two later and asked if I filed on the land yet. I said no. I didn't even know this guy's name, only that he owned an airplane. Well, it turned out to be Don Sheldon, one of the most famous pilots in Alaska. He said I should ride out on the train, he would show me where the land was.

I rode the train for free. When it stopped at Montana Creek, I got off and, at Don Sheldon's suggestion, checked in with Ralph Blankenship, who lived with his family in a tent on a homestead. They'd been through a winter there already. Land was available next to his.

It cost $10 to file on a 160-acre homestead at the Bureau of Land Management in Anchorage. I also filed on a 40-acre trade and manufacturing site near the railroad tracks. Don Sheldon's advice was good for me.

I was never able to prove up on the homestead. Joan didn't want to have any part of it. I sold out to a guy from Louisiana. After a couple of years I swapped the trade and manufacturing site for a sixteen-man squad tent. Can you imagine, I traded forty acres for a tent?

Working for the Alaska Railroad kept me going, but being laid off each winter was tough. One winter I worked on a drilling rig. Another winter the whole family went to Modesto, California. We saw a chalkboard sign offering jobs for "Grade A milkers." I walked up and I said, "If Grade A means you're good, then we qualify." The woman gave us cards that were like gold for getting us in the door at ranches.

I worked at the Producers Bar Twenty Dairy in Fresno. There were more than five hundred head of milk cows. I worked four hours on, eight off, four on wearing whites every time. They kept those uniforms and everything else clean. They had a four-hundred-seat amphitheatre. People came from all over the world to see the operation.

This was temporary work for me, spending winter in a warm climate. I knew I was going back to Anchorage in May when the railroad job opened up again. I was pleased to see a little sunshine for a few months, but I loved Alaska.

The Mountain View area of Anchorage represented the frontier that I had dreamed of. And it had an attitude—"We're going places. We're jumping." Everybody was upbeat. Water and sewer lines were being put in, and Mountain View was growing into an established city.

The first winter in Anchorage we went downtown to watch the Fur Rendezvous sled-dog races. The world championship was run over three days, with mushers racing twenty-five miles a day. Now it's called sprint mushing, but in 1960 it was just plain old mushing because there was no such thing as long-distance mushing. We enjoyed it and went to the races at Tudor Track, too.

The Fur Rondy winter carnival was a spectacle. It had a fur auction and all kinds of social events. People came into town from Bush Alaska. It was big. Dog teams ran down the main street on snow trucked in for the race. After the long winter we went to every event. You didn't want to miss a thing.

We didn't plan to race at first, but that winter we adopted a dog. Rick was in elementary school and wanted a pet. Someone in Spenard was giving away half-grown puppies. So the first Mackey dog was a husky we got for free. We named it Yukon.

We had one of those Flexible Flyer sleds, a little one about two and one-half feet long. I fastened Yukon to the sled, Rick sat on it, and I'd run down the street. The dog chased me, pulling Rick. In the beginning the dog ran a few feet and stopped, but after a while I had to run to catch him. Later I tied a rope to the back of the sled and ran behind it. When I got tired, I put on the brakes. That worked pretty well.

Of course one dog was not enough. It never is. If you're destined to mush, kennel expansion occurs naturally, even though you don't know you're building a kennel.

Our second winter in Anchorage, I had six dogs. The dogcatcher gave us some of his strays. We had a deal. Every dog that looked as if it might be a sled dog he brought to me instead of the pound. I got to keep the dog for a few days and check it out. If I thought it was going to work out, I'd keep it.

That's how it started for us. At that point Mackey mushing was Rick and I. He was the oldest. The other kids were still too young. I probably was more into mushing than Rick at first. We never dreamed one day we would have a major-league dog team like those famous mushers who were winning the races. Dr. Roland Lombard of Wayland, Massachusetts, and Alaskans George Attla and Gareth Wright were the main contenders for the big prizes. They seemed to live in a different world.

Little did we know how important dog mushing would become and how our lives would come to be dominated by it.

Me and leaders Teller and Skipper leaving the dog lot at Wasilla

People vs. dogs in Anchorage

When the earthquake hit there was a tremendous BOOM! The ground heaved so much that the trees were perpendicular. My first thought was that the Russians had dropped a bomb.

One of my earliest sprint teams in February 1968.

WHEN THE MACKEY KENNEL reached three dogs, I built Rick a sled. I put him in the basket, stood on the back runners, and we set out on trips from Mountain View. We crossed the new Glenn Highway, which had been rerouted around Fort Richardson, mushed along the gas line, and entered Tudor Track. Then we turned around and retraced our course.

We mushed ten or twelve miles with three dogs pulling the two of us. We didn't know then we were working the dogs too hard.

Soon the excitement of the annual Rendezvous sled dog races rubbed off on us. Rick was eight when he mushed competitively with a three-dog team.

He won his first race on a three-and-one-half-mile course, setting a record that lasted for years. The head of the junior mushers organization came up to me and said we needed to do this and that to become more competitive, and he said Rick won despite his lousy harnesses. This ticked me off. I had made those harnesses. Still, it was a lot of fun, and I thought I might try racing, too.

Before I could get started, though, we had to deal with a little problem. In 1962, a neighbor took us to court claiming our dogs made too much noise and were annoying the neighborhood. Her kitchen window looked across her next-door neighbor's yard into our back yard. The city attorney and a policeman came to the house and told us this Mrs. Snodgrass had complained seventeen times, and that they had to do *something*. And I was working with the woman's husband at the railroad!

At the time, we had six or seven dogs and each had its own wired-in kennel box. But when you took them out, hooked them up, and fed them, they barked like any dogs would. I didn't know what to do. The city people were apologetic, but they pursued the complaints.

I found an attorney, Jim Merbs, who was the head of the Anchorage Retriever Club. He loved dogs and believed in my cause. He charged me his minimum fee, $75, but later refunded the money. The crux of the case against me was a law prohibiting anybody from harboring an animal that was an annoyance to the neighborhood.

The city attorney thought it was going to be cut and dried. But my attorney said he didn't care how long it took to defend us because we were in the right. The whole neighborhood turned out in court. Merbs soon had Mrs. Snodgrass howling like a dog on the witness stand. He ridiculed her without mercy. The court recognized that everybody in the courtroom was there on my behalf. The judge suggested the city revise the wording of the animal-control law because one person did not constitute a "neighborhood." I was found not guilty.

Soon after that I became a serious musher. On a trip to Fairbanks I bought a leader for $150. It was a nice little dog, and we bred it.

I had a little more money by then. I was still employed by the Alaska Railroad and had progressed up from a job in the freight shed to being chief operations timekeeper. I kept the time cards for the conductors and brakemen. It was a job where you wore a suit and tie. But I wore my leather boots, too, because I wasn't going to give in to the dress code completely. The work was indoors. That was another drawback. One day I looked out the window and asked myself, "What am I doing in here?"

An opportunity arose to get on with the ironworkers. I was about to give thirty days' notice to the railroad when the Good Friday Earthquake struck in March 1964. That was the greatest natural disaster in Alaska history. It was the biggest earthquake ever in North America, and the tidal waves killed people all the way down the coast to California. There was terrible devastation in Anchorage and all over Southcentral Alaska.

When the earthquake hit, I was stepping through the front door of our new home on the south side of Anchorage. Rick handed me a bundle of harnesses as we planned to ride out to Eagle River and run dogs. The kids were all ready to go when there was a tremendous BOOM! The refrigerator slid from one side of the kitchen to the other—about twenty feet. I didn't get knocked down, probably because I stood in a doorway. I couldn't believe my eyes. The ground was heaving so violently that the trees swung back and forth like windshield wipers.

As the crow flies, we were not far from Fort Richardson and Elmendorf Air Force Base, and my first thought was, "The Russians dropped a bomb." I thought we were under attack. This was a few years after the Cuban missile crisis. Anchorage bases had been on high alert and even then we were required to carry survival gear in the trunk of the car.

We went outside to look at the damage. Our 1953 Ford had rolled over onto its side. And the quake wasn't over. By this time we were laying down in the gravel driveway holding onto each other. Suddenly, the ground split open, sending a crack right up the driveway—it must have been about four feet wide. Then, with a loud clapping sound, the fissure slammed shut.

The power of that earthquake was unbelievable. It measured 9.2 on the Richter scale. Clyde Sturdevant, who lived across the street, had a shop in his Quonset hut. He had broken his leg working on the new Chugiak High School, and it was in a cast. He was coming out the door of his house heading for the shop when an upheaval threw him seventeen feet! He had a ninety-foot well that flat disappeared. He never did find it. Nearby, a fissure opened up exposing another neighbor's septic tank, then crashed together again, rupturing the tank and sending its contents all over his house. Oh, man.

Clyde had a fireplace, so we all went over there, started a fire, and turned on the radio. Volunteers with first-aid experience were being asked to come to Providence Hospital. I had been on the rescue squad back in New Hampshire and, since all of us were fine, I took off. That didn't set too well with my wife, though.

The Army took over in Anchorage almost instantly, it seemed. Soldiers patrolled to prevent looting and set up bread and water stations. They gave cholera shots, too.

Providence Hospital was chaos. Many people were injured, though few deaths occurred in Anchorage. A lot of heroic things happened. One doctor who had lost a member of his family stayed on duty and operated on injured people for many hours.

I wasn't called on for first aid. Initially, all I did was keep order and comfort people who were dazed and hurt.

The next day there was an aftershock that seemed almost as strong as the original quake. Later there was damage when the gas lines were turned back on. It ignited some fires and people were killed.

After the earthquake, there was little railroad left in Southcentral Alaska. It was badly damaged. Nearly a week after the big shake I drove the first truckload of supplies to Portage, south of Anchorage. Fort Richardson soldiers walked along the highway in front of me. When we got to the Twenty Mile River, we saw that the highway bridge was out. But the railroad bridge was intact and I backed the truck across it. The Army unloaded the truck for the people awaiting rescue. A few had been evacuated by helicopter, but most were stranded.

After the emergency eased, I told my boss I was quitting. He said I couldn't afford to leave the railroad. I didn't like his attitude so I got on my high horse and walked right out with no notice. I felt badly not leaving on better terms.

Between the court case in 1962 and the earthquake two years later we had moved to South Anchorage where it was less congested. Even though I won the case, I could see what was coming: Somebody else would come along and protest about all the dogs and I'd be back in court. It happened that way all over Anchorage. New people moved in and raised a stink. Dog teams were driven out by growth. When I moved to the 72nd Street area, it was all wooded. Of course, now it's all houses, condominiums, and apartments.

When I moved I got to know Dick Tozier, who practically ran the Rendezvous. I'd be at Tozier's house for meetings, and they needed people to help. So I jumped right in. I volunteered to help smooth trails for the sled dog races. One year I was given the wheel-dog award for contributions to mushing.

Given that I was hanging out in the mushing community, it was inevitable that I would become a racer. I entered the Fur Rendezvous open class for the first time in 1965, finishing last. But I beat six others who scratched. One of those was Earl Norris, a two-time champion.

At the draw, I had picked a starting spot right in front of George Attla. In the 1960s, Attla and Doc Lombard were kings of the roost. The battle for the championship was often between them. George eventually won ten world championships, more than anyone else, and this was George in his prime,

We started the race at two-minute intervals and I was nervous. I had twelve or fourteen dogs. I was just expecting George to catch me and pass me right away. If dog teams pass each other too closely they can get tangled. That was my worry. I was hoping I would be on open ground and not on tight trail when Attla came up on me. But it didn't play out that way. As soon as I entered a narrow, wooded stretch of trail there was Attla coming up fast behind. What to do? There was no room. George and I are friends now, but he didn't know me then. He came roaring up and yelled, "Get that bunch of crap out of my way!"

I thought I had been doing well! This encounter made me feel about two inches high, I didn't want to goof him up, though, and I managed to pull aside.

That year Lombard won the race. After three days of racing, I was fifty-six minutes behind eighteenth place. Later, a rule was passed that set a time limit for completion of the course.

There are people today running middle- and long-distance races who shouldn't be running because they're not qualified. Back then, I was inexperienced, too. In those days, the race organizers just wanted bodies. That was my first race and I was excited to be in it.

Iron work and dog mushing

I couldn't refuse. So I cut off a sliver and chewed and chewed. But I couldn't swallow the fermented muscle from the fin of a seal. Oh it was vile.

I got to know Joe Redington working in Southwest Alaska.

I STARTED WORKING iron in 1964. The earthquake played a big role in my transition away from the Alaska Railroad. I was all set to join the Ironworkers union anyway, and there was so much rebuilding to be done.

I helped build the post-earthquake Alaska, traveling all over the state helping to fix buildings and to put up new ones. I worked in Ketchikan, Juneau, Sitka, and Kodiak, to name a few places. I spent a whole summer in Seward working on the new railroad dock, the new round house, and the harbormaster's house.

I had no background as an ironworker. My neighbor got me started in welding. That got me in the door. Then I went through welding school. Once I became a certified welder I was set.

The funny thing is that the first building I welded on was the welding school itself on Fireweed Lane in Anchorage. My earliest work was in Anchorage, but then the union got a request for five men in Seldovia. And I was off, assigned to a new place. I helped put in a new digester at the Ketchikan Pulp Mill.

Most were summer jobs because that's the basic construction season in Alaska the weather dictates. But there was winter work too. One winter job was welding on the construction of a new natural gas building on Spenard Road. It was the first Visqueen-heated building I had seen used for winter construction in the Anchorage area.

I loved being sent to the Bush. It was a great experience. I liked visiting a community, doing a job, and then going on to another new community. It beat punching the clock and going through the same door every day.

At first, I made friends mostly with co-workers, especially in the bigger cities like Ketchikan and Sitka. I liked Sitka with its historic Russian influence. I visited the Pioneer Home and talked with some of the old-timers, who told colorful stories about the Gold Rush. I ate that stuff up.

I'll never forget the fishing in Ketchikan. We caught halibut and salmon. And I used to put out crab pots. It was a time in my life when I liked to party and drink so I spent a lot of time in bars with the guys. These were fun times, but sometimes the partying got out of hand.

We'd finish our shift and somebody would say, "Tonight we're going to get some sleep." Then, somebody would say, "Maybe just one more beer?" Then it would be a couple more beers and something to eat. Before you knew it, four o'clock in the morning rolled around and we'd get an hour of sleep, a shower, and go back to work again.

In 1967, I hooked on to a project on the Drift River in Cook Inlet building an offshore loading platform. I started there on May 1 and didn't get home until Thanksgiving. That was pretty much the end of my first marriage. Being away took a toll.

I was out of town a lot. I did iron work in more Bush communities than I ever mushed through—Golovin, Unalakleet, St. Michael, Galena, McGrath, Anvik, and Holy Cross. I worked in a lot of those places later when I became a contractor on my own.

This was my first exposure to Alaska's Native communities, where I got to know both Eskimos and Athabascans. I was most impressed with the industrious people in the communities on the Bering Sea Coast—Nome, St. Michael, Unalakleet, White Mountain, and Golovin.

Life in many of these villages revolved around fishing. In Golovin, I worked for the Community Enterprise Development Corporation, a federal grant program, and at the fish-processing plant. I got work through Joe Redington Sr., who later became known as "Father of the Iditarod." Joe became a close friend, and you'll hear a lot more about him. At any rate, I worked with and for Joe.

The development corporation sent me to Golovin to find out why the fish-processing place there wasn't making a go of it. Millions of dollars had been put into it.

I discovered the problem—the plant was inundated with salmon and didn't have enough workers to process them. They received tons of kings, silvers, and reds. The plant could have processed as much as one million pounds of fish in a season, but there were only 123 people in the community including the elderly and children, and there wasn't enough labor available.

The plant tried to hire people to come in and work but the workers had nowhere to stay. So I built a 150-bed camp and recruited workers from Elim, White Mountain, and Nome.

I fell in love with White Mountain, not knowing it would become a key resting checkpoint in the last stretch of a world-famous race that had not yet been conceived. The country is absolutely beautiful. The river is so clear you can see the fish swimming in the water. And you can get into a skiff and in thirty minutes be in salt water at Golovin Bay. The surrounding country has good trapping, hunting, and fishing. I always said when I retired White Mountain was where I would go. I guess I haven't retired because I haven't made it there yet.

One job I had in St. Michael was putting up the Chevron building that Jerry Austin runs. That was years before Jerry became an Iditarod Hall of Fame musher. Everywhere I went in those small villages I got to know people.

In Galena, I met Sidney Huntington. He was on the state game board forever and he's the father of the late Carl Huntington, the only musher to win both the Fur Rendezvous and the Iditarod. Carl and I ran together in the 1974 Iditarod for a long ways. I always seemed to gravitate to the elders because I loved to hear their stories and all about their ways of doing things.

The father of Clara Austin, Jerry's wife, was a chief of the village in St. Michael at one time. He told me this story. As chief he was responsible for providing meat, so he went out to hunt caribou. But he got lost. He stopped to consider the situation, then asked himself, "Which way was the wind blowing when the grass froze?" He dug down beneath the snow and looked at how the grass was laying, and from this he could tell east from west. He regained his bearings and found his way home.

Whenever I went to Nome and visited Howard Farley and his wife, Julie, they took me to see her elderly father, Leo Panuck, who was an ivory carver. The last time I saw him he was sitting there with a cigar-like substance in his mouth. He would take a knife, cut off a chunk, and chew it.

I said, "Mr. Panuck, what is that?" Dumb question. Instead of answering, he cut off a piece and gave it to me. I couldn't refuse. That would have been rude. I remember Julie looking at me with a warning look in her eyes.

I stuck this thing between my teeth and cut off a sliver and chewed and chewed. Finally, I excused myself, went into the bathroom, and spit it out. I couldn't swallow the dam thing. It was the fermented muscle of the flipper from a seal. Oh, it was *vile*. Oh boy.

Even though I worked in all of these places for years and absorbed much Native culture, I felt like a tourist. It was a long time before I considered myself an Alaskan. Probably the two biggest things I contributed in Alaska were helping start the Iditarod and winning it, and building up the Coldfoot truck stop.

Members of my family made contributions, too. When I was away from home, someone had to raise the kids and, frankly, that wasn't as high on my list as it should have been. Right or wrong, my job came first. I did iron work from 1964 until 1981 when I went to Coldfoot. I can't think of a day I didn't enjoy getting up and going to work. However, sometimes ironwork conflicted with my aspirations to become a competitive dog musher.

I ran the Rendezvous into the early 1970s—even finished eleventh a couple of times—but I never was going to train as single-mindedly as the top mushers. I had a job. And when I wasn't away on the job, I spent a lot of time in town helping the mushing organization, following Joe Redington Sr.'s lead.

Once, in the mid-1960s, I was on a job in Seldovia. We were putting up an apartment building-store complex. Rick, who was eleven or twelve, helped train my dogs for me as the Fur Rendezvous races approached. I was far from town, but I wanted to be part of the Rondy.

I had done quite a bit of training before the Seldovia job started in midwinter. But the weather was bad. That's one thing about working in villages that are off the road system. Except for Southeast, with its state ferry routes, you've got to fly. Frequently, small planes can't get in and out of those remote airstrips, due to snowstorms, extreme cold, or lousy visibility.

I was supposed to fly from Seldovia to Homer several days before the race and then catch a connecting flight to Anchorage. But the pilot, Bob Gruber of Cook Inlet Aviation, told me conditions were too poor to fly passengers. This dragged on and on. I was stranded. Finally, Bob said there was one way he could get me to Homer. If he hired me as an employee then I wouldn't be a paying passenger. Even though weather conditions were under the margin, he "hired" me and we took off in his little Cessna 185.

It was cloudy and snowing. I had lost my cushion and no longer hoped to get into town early for the race. In fact, I had to get to Homer right then, or I wouldn't make the Anchorage flight at all. Bob said he didn't think we'd make it, but he'd radio ahead. The connecting flight waited twenty minutes for us.

In Anchorage, I grabbed a cab, changed my clothes in the back seat, and got out on Fourth Avenue near the startling line. My family was there waiting with my dog team. I stepped onto the runners just in time. I've often thought, how many planes would wait for you today?

It would be nice to say that I placed high in the standings after all that, but the truth is that I never did well in the Rendezvous. After my debut in nineteenth place, I finished fourteenth in 1966 and fifteenth two years later. That was typical. I had my share of misadventures, too.

Gilman's Bakery used to be located right on Cordova Street a few hundred yards past the starting line. One year my dogs came around the corner just as someone opened the front door of the bakery. The dogs bolted right inside as far as they could get, all of the dogs. They liked the smell, I guess. The sled got stuck in the doorway.

The only thing I could do was tie off on a power pole, then go inside and get each dog, one by one. I was there so long that soon TV cameras were rolling and hundreds of people gathered to watch. Doc Lombard went by me and he had started fourteen positions back. That's twenty-eight minutes.

Neither my dogs nor I got fed, either. I deserved a loaf of bread, at least. Until then I was just a name on a list of starters. After that, people cheered us on the course. For a long time people would tease me by asking, "Hey, Dick, got any doughnuts with you?"

One year I followed Joee Redington out. Joee was going in circles, and I was right behind him. We were going towards Cordova to get to the route leading out of town but instead we turned onto Fifth Avenue, went a couple of blocks, and came right back out on Fourth. Then, looking for a short cut back to Cordova Street, we ended up going all the way around *again*! Oh, it was chaotic.

Getting serious about mushing

Joe Redington offered to train a leader for me.
So we made a deal. For a one-hundred-dollar bill,
he would train a dog to "gee" and "haw." And he did.

Me and three of my children—Bill, Becky, and Rick.

IN SPRINT RACING, the Mackey kids were much better than their dad.

I was more into the social aspect of it and having a good time. The kids raced on Saturday, more often than not with the same dogs I ran on Sunday. Maybe the dogs were a little bit tired before I started.

When I moved to the south side of Anchorage—"rural" we called it then —Dick Tozier and I became neighbors. He had a large kennel. He ran dogs, but didn't race. The neighborhood was a hotbed of mushing. Orville Lake, whom they've named a race after, lived out there. And when Doc Lombard came to town, that's where he stayed. Charlie Belford, another top racer and Rendezvous champion, came from Massachusetts every winter and stayed with Dick.

So I moved in with the big boys, although that was unintended. I ended up near them because that's where land was available. The first year I lived there, there wasn't much snow. When Charlie Belford arrived, Tozier told him I would show him where to go. I took him out to Eklutna Lake, and then every year he came to Alaska I trained with him.

Bill Sturdevant was a junior musher. He and his dad, Clyde, who got me into the ironworkers, were friends of George Attla. George stayed at the Sturdevants' when he came to town, so he took Bill under his wing. Since I was around, I'd train with him, too. I learned a lot about dogs from George, and we became good friends.

I mostly had dogs that were saved from the pound. Once I settled into the south part of town, I tried to get more serious about mushing, so I went to see Earl Norris. Later, Earl moved way out of town to Willow on the Parks Highway, where he bred Siberian Huskies and tutored many beginners over the years. But at that time his homestead was located where University Center Mall later was built.

Earl was a two-time Rondy world champion and his wife, Natalie, was a champion of the women's race. In 1947, Earl and his dog team carried supplies up to Mount McKinley for a climb led by Dr. Bradford Washburn. On that climb, Barbara Washburn became the first woman to reach the summit of Mount McKinley, and the expedition got lots of attention in the movies and in *National Geographic*. It made Earl famous, and he lived off it. He worked hard, too. He raised and sold lots of dogs. It was a big deal to have an Earl Norris-bred dog.

Earl said to me, "You want to get into dog mushing?" I told him I did, but I was poor-mouthing the idea, too. I told him I didn't have much money. Dog mushers never seem to have enough money. He and Natalie talked it over and gave me six dogs. Boy, they were alligators. You talk about fighters. Still, that was a major upgrade in my dog lot.

By the late 1960s and early 1970s, all the kids were racing. Rick was first because he was the oldest. Becky and Bill followed him. One year Rick competed in the seven-dog class, Becky in the five, and Bill in the three, if I recall. And they all won their races. I was a proud poppa.

The population growth of Anchorage finally caught up to us by 1970 and we moved to Wasilla. The trails were closing up in Anchorage. There was more land and usually more snow in Wasilla. I bought ten acres in the Rainbow Lake area, about eight miles north of Wasilla proper, and moved a mobile home onto the property. That meant I was about sixty miles from Anchorage the way the old roads ran. By then I was divorced and married to wife number two, Kathie Bliss. My two sons from that marriage are Lance and Jason. Lance has just begun Iditarod racing.

Wasilla was more rural then. This was before the Knik River bridges were built. From Wasilla you had to cut over to Palmer to drive into Anchorage. I bet there were only about five of us in the Wasilla area who commuted to Anchorage. If you saw an unfamiliar car on the road you wondered who it was, that's how little traffic there was.

The Mackeys did a lot of mushing with the Aurora Dog Mushers Club out in the Mat-Su Valley, but we were active in Anchorage, too. It's difficult to make young people understand how important the Rendezvous was back then. Quite a few Iditarod mushers got their start in sprint mushing. You'll see names on the list of Rendezvous competitors from thirty years ago who are still active today. Bill Cotter is one—he's still racing up near the front in the Iditarod. Jerry Riley is another.

The Fur Rendezvous is where I met Joe Redington. Joe offered to train a leader for me. I had a good dog that was not very responsive to commands. I was working, and Joe said he had lots of free time. So we made a deal. For a one-hundred-dollar bill he said he'd train that dog to "gee" and "haw," and he did.

When it came to Rendezvous, Joe was not much more successful than I was. He was considered a bit of an outlaw. His boys Joee Jr., Raymie, and Tim were racing at the same time as my kids, but the Redington boys were considered to be a wild bunch. You know, as in "that wild bunch that lives up in Knik."

I'm not sure why I took a liking to Joe, and he to me. But we became close friends. He was nearly fifteen years older than me. When my dad passed away in 1973—the day the first Iditarod started—Joe sort of became my surrogate dad.

Actually, I didn't know my father had died until I reached Nome. My mother got hold of Dick Tozier and informed him, but he wasn't supposed to break the news until I reached the finish line.

Later, Joe was the best man at my wedding when I married Cathy Thompson in 1982. I used to visit him in Knik and at his homestead on Flathorn Lake.

I kept moving north. My first home was Anchorage. Then it was Wasilla. Then Coldfoot. The only time I moved south was leaving Coldfoot to settle in Nenana.

I've been a cold-weather person my whole life. Being brought up in New England, I always liked the cold. And I hated rain. The season I spent working iron in Seward I never went a shift without rain gear.

Ketchikan was always soggy. One time it didn't rain for ten days, and a water emergency was declared. They didn't have reservoirs. You can't do the work all bundled up in rain gear. By the same token, you can't work on the North Slope all bundled up in the winter, either, even if I didn't appreciate that at first. My philosophy is if it's winter, let's have a good snow. Maybe that made me a natural for mushing.

Some people complain about the lack of daylight in the winter. I never minded the dark when I was working. You deal with it. When I trained dogs, I arranged my schedule to take advantage of what daylight there was. It used to be a problem for the kids after school. They didn't have much time to run dogs before dark. We played a little game, seeing how fast they could get home after school.

I admit that as I got older, with injuries I've had, the cold bothered me more. I don't like running dogs at 40 below zero anymore. It never bothered me before. When I lived in Coldfoot, 40 below was the cutoff. It wasn't so much me as the dogs. My youngest daughter, Kris, used to go out with me at Coldfoot and she hated it. She was freezing. It didn't bother me then. Now it does.

I was skinny. I was five-foot-ten and weighed 160 pounds. I had no extra fat. So I had to put on extra clothes to keep warm. If it got colder, I put on more clothes. And so on.

Mushing was one thing, but it seemed colder when we were building an oil platform in Prudhoe Bay. You ate and ate and ate. They fed you like a king. But working outdoors burned up so many calories I never gained more than five pounds.

When I was young I had dogs for hunting, but Alaska sled dogs are different. They are great athletes and most make good household pets. They're affectionate, given the opportunity to be. And they're adaptable, easy to care for, and they don't often mind the cold. They're just one heck of a dog!

Racing dogs used to be much bigger. When Joee Redington Jr. won the Rondy in 1965 he had two dogs, Happy and Windy, who weighed nearly eighty pounds apiece. Now the sprint racing dogs are much smaller, maybe forty-five pounds, and even Iditarod dogs are more likely to be fifty-five or sixty pounds. Through breeding, mushers found that smaller dogs are better suited to long-distance running.

When I started racing, there were two kinds of dogs—the Alaska village husky and the Siberian husky. The dogs I got from Earl Norris were Siberians. He always has been a proponent of that breed. Siberians are beautiful dogs. They have a regal bearing. People outside of Alaska suppose that's what an Alaska husky should look like, a dog with a masked face and black and white or gray markings and blue eyes. But the Siberians don't run as fast as Alaska huskies. In racing circles you can get into an argument over Siberians versus other dogs, but I think it's universally accepted today that crossbred Alaska huskies are better than purebred Siberians in racing.

When I started my own breeding, I crossed a registered Siberian with a registered black Lab. The kids kept the line going. Many dog generations have gone by, but you still can trace some of today's Mackey dogs to those first two.

Sprint racing at its peak

*On the cross-country trips into the Denali country
I bonded with the dogs. The Alaska Range was visible
in all its glory and the land was open and immense.*

I loved cross-country mushing even before the Iditarod.

Bill Devine

YOU CAN'T MUSH thousands of miles without the occasional mis-adventure. Everybody loses a team now and then.

I had just bought a new snap that connected the bridle to the gang line. The piece—they don't use them now—was called a bull snap. I was starting one of my everyday training runs at Campbell Airstrip on a trail that ran to the Tudor Track, where most of the sprint races took place. It was my first run. The bull snap was defective, and broke the same day I bought it.

I had a dozen or so dogs hooked up. When I yelled, "Go," away they went. But I didn't go with them. There I was standing on the runners of the sled left behind. The dogs disappeared. What can you do? I ran for home, about two miles away, and I jumped into my truck to look for those dogs.

That is a musher's worst nightmare. Lucky for me, the dogs did run to the track, and a musher there stopped them. But they got into tangles and started fighting and got tore up pretty bad.

This Good Samaritan brought the injured dogs to Orville Lee's house, just beyond the clubhouse, and he took them to Bob Scott, the veterinarian. By the time I reached the track most of my dogs were tied up. But Orville had left for the vet. Bob Scott was stitching up two of them when I finally caught up. Both recovered.

It's worse, of course, if the dogs take off and leave you when you're in the middle of nowhere. Usually your first concern is for the dogs, not yourself. The first rule of mushing is never let go of the sled, even if you're being dragged. One time, though, I was going to be smashed into a tree. I was being bounced along holding on, but finally I let go to save myself.

In that case, I knew someone in front of me in all probability would catch the team. That's what happened. If you're training a rookie with your team you tell them that they'd better have a piece of the sled handle in their hand if they come home without the dogs.

There was no Iditarod in the 1960s, and I always felt sprint races were too short. Some races were ten miles, and your week's racing might end in thirty minutes. After that, you were down at the track just BSing with the bunch. The socializing took more time than the race. You spent the afternoon and evening out there for a half-hour race. Never mind the driving time to races out of town.

What I enjoyed, in late October or early November, was using my dogs to hunt behind Sourdough Lodge out on the Richardson Highway, or on the Denali Highway out of Paxson. I went out after the first snowfall when I worked for the railroad and had been laid off for the season. Most of the construction wrapped up by mid-October, too, and then it was dog time. This worked out great.

I spent weeks at a time mushing around exploring the backcountry and hunting caribou. That was my true enjoyment with the dogs. And I got my caribou. I've always been a good shot. Son Bill came with me and somehow he can see game behind him. I still call him Swivel Head. But I'm the one who shot the caribou to feed the family.

On those long trips I bonded with the dogs. The longer I was out the more I liked it. That Denali country is awesome with the Alaska Range visible in all its glory and the feeling of openness and the immensity of the land.

Those long trips made me more inclined to back the Iditarod when it came along, more so than the core group of sprint mushers who were Alaska's athlete heroes of the time. In fact, some of the Anchorage sprint mushers ridiculed me for supporting the Iditarod, which was seen as a threat to the sprint races. Even though I hung around with a sprint-mushing crowd, I was more compatible with Joe Redington, who liked to take long backcountry dog trips, too.

Dr. Roland Lombard came from Wayland, Massachusetts, a suburb of Boston, and showed us a new way of life that you could make pay off, too. When Doc and Charlie Belford came north at first there was a feeling of "We're Alaskans and we know what we're doing." When Doc Lombard entered the Rendezvous the first time, he drove Siberians and didn't do so well. Then he bought some Alaska dogs and he became a tremendous competitor. He adapted quickly.

Although there was a faction that rooted for George Attla and the other Alaskans, others rooted for Doc Lombard. He was a perfect gentleman. George won ten world championships. Lombard won eight titles, and people loved him. Despite being an outsider challenging Alaskans, people felt he contributed so much to racing that it was OK that he won.

Doc never volunteered information. But if you asked him a question, he would tell you everything he knew pertaining to that question. He was a veterinarian who taught us a lot about dog care. He understood the workings of dogs better than we did and he generously shared his knowledge.

George Attla won races before Lombard came north and George won after Lombard retired. But in the 1960s when they went head to head was the most exciting time for the Fur Rendezvous. Gareth Wright was still contending, too, and Joee Redington Jr. won a title. And there were always Native mushers coming in representing the villages.

It was exciting to be part of it. We didn't know this was the Rendezvous at its peak. I developed a following, not through any conscious effort and not because I was very good. If you were personable, happy go lucky and were a regular, people knew you. I suffered some terrible problems on the trail, but I was always happy out there, and the fans followed my misadventures. You developed an identity—"Dick Mackey, he's the guy who always runs the Fur Rendezvous. I see him race every year."

Much later, when I won the Iditarod, people wrote letters to the editor and said things like, "Isn't it great when a good guy wins?" The Rondy is why they felt they knew me.

The regulars were received warmly in Fairbanks for the North American Sled Dog Championship, too. I raced in Fairbanks once, in the late 1960s. It was different terrain from the Rendezvous—a little easier, I thought—and I finished in the top ten.

In 1968, I drove to a race in St. Paul, Minnesota. It was the only time I ever raced outside of Alaska. I was going through a divorce and needed money. I thought I could sell some dogs.

I took eighteen dogs with me and sold a half dozen or so. I got $300 for a good dog, which was a lot of money at the time. In fact, given my history with fifty-dollar cars, I figured each dog was worth six automobiles. I drove some junkers.

I drove non-stop from Anchorage to Whitehorse. That's 750 miles. Oh man, was it cold. The Yukon can be colder than Fairbanks. I got a hotel room for the night and picketed my dogs across the street next to a school. Someone called up the *Whitehorse Star*, and the newspaper made a big deal about me traveling to Minnesota. Got a nice writeup.

Farther down the Alaska Highway, I had an accident. I had picked up a hitchhiker near Watson Lake and being dead tired, I let him drive. Next thing I knew we were off the side of the road, and the dog box had flown off the back of the truck. Turns out he fell asleep, too.

I ended up in the hospital. I already had a bad back from the truck accident a decade before in New Hampshire. But I couldn't stay in the hospital. I had a race to run. I was almost immobilized from the pain, but I made it to Minnesota.

Jerry Riley, who lives a few miles down the road from me in Nenana, and who won the Iditarod in 1976, was the only other Alaskan competing. The other mushers, about seventy in all, were mostly from Canada.

The race consisted of three heats of eighteen miles each. I was totally out of it the first day. I had to have somebody hook up my team. I just stood on the sled runners and somehow came in tenth.

I was not the only one in the family who was accident-prone around dogs, either. Daughter Becky broke her left ankle twice. She was about ten when she broke it going out of the dog lot, hitting a tree, and a year later she broke it again doing the same thing.

The second time was alarming. Because Becky was young and still growing, the doctor was concerned the break might cause permanent problems. But it didn't. I cut the tree down.

Back then, the sport was in the good hands of Earl Norris, Dick Tozier, and Orville Lake, all great dog men. They loved sprint racing and were dedicated to it.

It's fitting that the Tudor Track was renamed the Tozier Track following the death of Dick Tozier. Dick was my role model for being a race marshal. I developed my philosophy from him. I believe the ultimate success of the race marshal and others who organize sled dog races is based on what they do to help every musher and dog cross the finish line within the confines of the rules.

You have to enforce the rules but you have to be fair. There seems to be more leeway now for officials to use judgment. It may be that the growth of sponsorships helped. Races have to answer to that. If I bring a team to a race with a group of corporate people who support me, and one stupid thing gets me disqualified, hey, come on now. A penalty is much more acceptable than disqualification. You're still in there. You finish.

I believe Alaska as a whole has become less open over the past forty years. There's less connectedness between people. I always take a special pride in being Alaskan.

A lot of that has disappeared. Maybe more people come to Alaska now because their employer transfers them. The ones who keep the spirit alive come north for the hunting or fishing and because Alaska is still the Last Frontier. They still feel that northern kinship.

When I moved to Wasilla, the Rainbow Bar was the community hall. Once a month we all went there and celebrated with everyone who happened to have a birthday. That's where we had our Christmas and Thanksgiving dinners. Few of us had families in Alaska, and there was no other place. In those days you accepted everybody at face value for what they were.

I remember a woman who moved to Wasilla, and the first thing she wanted to do was have a community meeting because we needed to put up a stop sign. Oh yeah, and wouldn't it be nice if we had a streetlight? I said, "Lady, you just left all that in Anchorage. Why don't you go back there?"

She reminded me of the people in Anchorage who had moved in next door and then complained about the dogs.

Getting behind a big idea

Support for a race to Nome came from a bunch of people at a place called "The Warehouse." First time I met some of them, they were buck-naked!

Joe Redington and I posted Iditarod Trail markers.

AN IDITAROD—not the Iditarod Trail Sled Dog Race as we know it—was held in 1967. Little did we know how the idea would grow.

In 1967, Dorothy Page, who was in charge of Wasilla's celebration of the 100th anniversary of Alaska's purchase from Russia, went to Joe Redington and asked if there was a way to incorporate a race on the old Iditarod Trail.

The way Joe described it, she asked how much trail was available. The trail had fallen into disuse, was covered with brush, and was pockmarked with ruts. It's not the comparatively smooth dog sled highway we think of today. Joe said it was possible to have a race, but that only twenty-eight miles of the trail was open between Knik and Big Lake.

That's what determined the distance. The race was announced as three heats of twenty-eight miles.

By then, Joe and I were friendly and when I heard there was going to be a race I asked if there was anything I could do to help. I knew little about the Iditarod Trail other than it had its roots in gold mining. I'd read some of the history.

When Joe said twenty-eight miles were open, that wasn't quite true. Even that stretch needed work. Joe's son, Joee, and I went out and cut a mile's worth of trail over Nine-Mile Hill with chain saws. Thick willows and birch had fallen over the trail, and the brush was dense. Some of the trunks of the downed trees were five inches in diameter.

Actually, the first thing we had to do was *find* the trail. Homesteads covered portions of the trail. We found the original markings on Nine-Mile Hill and could see the spots where mushers had lowered freight sleds down the steep hill. Joee and I worked for two days. It was winter work and it was cold. Other volunteers worked on sections of the trail. Ed Carney sunk his Cat in the swamp out there, and it took a year to get it out.

There was a lot of excitement about this race because it was something different. It wasn't a true cross-country race like the Iditarod became, but it wasn't going around in circles on a local route, either. We had good prize money and the centennial had attracted big names in mushing from the Bush.

This was the first time I met Isaac Okleasik from Teller and Herbie Nayokpuk from Shishmaref, two superb racers. We clicked right off. Maybe it was because of my familiarity with some of the rural areas from my ironwork.

Isaac, who won the race, was a tremendous dog man. Bush mushers didn't have the background and depth of knowledge from professional veterinarians we have now, so they operated more by instinct. Well, Isaac had that instinct. He understood dogs.

Bush mushers were more seat-of-the-pants mushers then. They didn't have the fancy rigs with their names emblazoned on the side. They didn't have a lot of money. Heck, in those days no dog musher had money. For the most part, mushers were a poor, scroungy bunch. Even many Iditarod mushers don't have time for full-time jobs. It's like the old joke: I was driving down the road and saw this strange animal run across. Boy, it was the scroungiest, dirtiest animal you ever saw. So I shot it. Come to find out it was a *homesteader*.

In 1967, I met Dorothy Page. Dorothy came to be known as the Mother of the Iditarod for her devotion to the race and hard work. Dorothy was a history nut. The historical significance of doing something special on the Iditarod Trail was her cup of tea. She and her husband, Von, became good friends. She was highly opinionated, but a lot of us were. It was her way or the highway. If you stayed on her good side, she was a friend. But if you crossed her, you were not a friend, and she didn't get over it. Thankfully, I remained a friend.

Once she tossed out the idea of the 1967 Iditarod to Joe Redington, Joe got behind it and led the way in the mushing community. Dorothy pushed it in the newspaper and in her writings. She called people on the phone and she was influential.

There was a lot of excitement about the race. It was running dogs in the woods. It brought newcomers from the Bush who never tried the Fur Rendezvous. I wanted to be part of it. I was still working, so I didn't have the time to train seriously, but I was going to be a participant.

The first day, about twelve miles into the race, one of my dogs stepped into a hole and broke a leg. I carried the dog in the basket most of the first day. That didn't help my attitude. I finished near the back of the pack.

This was the number one centennial event, so people came out to watch. It was special, a one-time thing, never to happen again. Except in Dorothy's eyes. This new race became her passion. Soon it was Joe's too. He wanted to keep something going on the trail.

When the race was over, a meeting was called in Knik. I was there with Joe, Dick Tozier, Earl Norris, and others. Ten of us became charter members of the Iditarod Trailblazers. We each contributed $100 and made ourselves lifetime members. The idea was to have a startup fund for some kind of long-distance race. "Long distance" was an ill-defined term. We had just completed the longest race run since the old 400-mile All-Alaska Sweepstakes in Nome before 1920.

Some of us had gone off on our own for 100 miles, hunting and camping, but never in a race. Dorothy pushed to keep the use of the trail alive, and Joe jumped in with both feet. The original idea was to race from Anchorage to the old ghost town of Iditarod, a distance of about 500 miles. That was the goal.

An Iditarod Trail Committee was formed—I was not part of that group—and there was a half-hearted suggestion to repeat the 1967 race in 1968. A date was announced, but the event wasn't advertised very well. There was no snow, conditions were icy, and people were busy working. No race took place. After that a group of us decided if we were going to keep this thing going we'd better have a race in 1969. We put up as a purse the $1,000 we had collected from the Trailblazers. George Attla won the 1969 race. It wasn't as big-time as the 1967 race, though, and the momentum to hold an annual race on the Iditarod Trail was dwindling.

For a couple of years after that, there was just talk. I had moved to Wasilla by then, lived close to Joe, and we stayed in contact. We talked dogs all the time. We kept the strangest hours. If my phone rang around midnight, I'd pick it up and say, "What's up, Joe?" If his phone rang around midnight, he'd answer it by saying, "What are you doing, Dick?" We called each other frequently, mostly discussing dogs. And we saw each other at local races in the Big Lake area. By then there were enough races to keep us busy in the Mat-Su Valley so that we didn't drive to Anchorage as often.

In November 1972, my phone rang and Joe said, "Guess what?" He had found some volunteers and financial backing to put on a race. The support came from a bunch at a place in Anchorage called "The Warehouse." Joe thought they had some kind of loose Democratic Party affiliation, but really the group was pretty loose. They were more of a commune than a political outfit. First time I met some of the people there, they were *buck-naked!* They were into all kinds of oddball stuff.

In discussions with these volunteers, Joe said he wanted to put on a long-distance mushing race to Iditarod. Someone said, "Where the hell is Iditarod? Why don't you run to Nome? Everybody knows where Nome is."

So, Joe asked me, "What do you think about running to Nome?" And I said, "I'll be the second one to sign up." He said, "What do you mean?" And I said, "Haven't you signed up yet?" And we were off and running.

A day later, Joe called at two o'clock in the morning and said we had to meet at the Warehouse in eight hours. So Joe and I went down there and knocked at the door. A head stuck out to say hello and in the background naked women were scattering away from the door. Joe looked at me with that lopsided grin of his and said, "Ain't this something?"

Joe and I sat down with these people, and they promised to help. We were representing the dog community. It was the only meeting I attended there, though I know there were others with Joe and Tom Johnson and Gleo Hyck. Later, Governor Bill Egan called Joe and suggested that it would not be in the best interests of the race if meetings continued to be held at the Warehouse.

For the first time, though, I sensed there really would be a long-distance race across Alaska. We were going to mush to Nome.

Joe said that I should take charge of putting in the trail between Anchorage and Susitna Station and supervise signups. Get the word out to mushers all over. It took a lot of cooperation from people like Joe Delia in Skwentna, and Howard Farley in Nome, and numerous villages along the route to put in a trail. When Joe heard that the U.S. Army was going to test some snowmachines to determine the feasibility of using them as regular Army equipment, he enlisted their assistance.

We had all of that help and still, when we got ready to go in March of 1973, the Iditarod Trail was pretty rough—much rougher than what mushers are used to today. Many areas had no trail. Snowshoes were required equipment and, believe me, you walked miles in them.

After I drew my assignment from Joe, I went home and started pounding out a letter on my typewriter announcing the richest dog-mushing event in the history of the world. Joe Redington guaranteed a $50,000 purse and of course everyone thought he was crazy. We didn't even have rules yet, but he set that figure. I told people we were going March 3, that we were going from Anchorage to Nome, and that we were chasing $50,000 in prize money. That's about all we knew at the time.

The promise of a $50,000 purse got people's attention. It was unheard of. I took a letter down to Wasilla High School late one night and Vern Cherneski, a teacher and a musher, ran off copies on one of those old AB Dick machines. I mailed copies to every village in Interior Alaska—anywhere I knew there was a musher who had competed in the Rendezvous or the North American. Soon mushers were sending $300 entry fees to Von Page, the treasurer.

Not everybody thought this was a great idea, though. I was still involved with the Anchorage mushing club that put on the sprint races, and I was ridiculed for falling into step with the Iditarod people. Some of them thought it was a pipe dream because of the distance and the money. They doubted the race would materialize. But I knew it was going to happen.

In my spare time, I trained my dogs. I knew running ten miles two or three times a week wasn't enough training for a 1,000-mile race. So, I went out and trained all day, almost every day.

Yet none of us knew what we were doing. We didn't know how to prepare physically. What do you have for clothing? What do you have for food? George Attla was the first one to say you could run one hundred miles a day, so we'd be there in ten days. But we really didn't know how far it was from Anchorage to Nome. We knew it was more than 1,000 miles, but that was about it. We tacked on forty-nine miles for the forty-ninth state. That's how it came to be described as a race of 1,049 miles.

Ralston-Purina donated twenty tons of dog food, Purina Hi-Pro. We were feeding our teams the ultimate dog food. The best there was. The funny thing was, when the dog food arrived and was dispersed out along the trail, some people in the villages didn't know why this dog food was being shipped in.

There was no formal checkpoint system in place the way the Iditarod evolved later. Joe would just get on the telephone and tell people in a village that a shipment of dog food was on the way. "We're going to have a race come through there." Joe was persistent. He was a big-picture guy, but he didn't always follow up on the details. That was for somebody else to do most of the time.

Once Joe Redington set his mind to something, there was no deviation from it. His credo was, "It's going to work, we'll make it work." There was a core group, and Joe was the leader. Other people were just as dedicated, but he was the foreman of this outfit. Because the financial commitment was so great, and the fundraising was so difficult, everyone was happy to let Joe be the one out in front.

One day Joe and I were sitting around with someone who was not a musher, and the guy asked, "Do you think one person can do this?" Joe laughed and said maybe we should take our wives with us. It was a joke at first, but it became serious. Although no wives signed up to mush with their husbands to Nome, we wrote the rules to allow teams of two to work together on a single sled. That year one duo—brothers Robert and Owen Ivan—raced together, finishing sixteenth. It was the only year teams were allowed.

Joe and I wrote the original thirteen rules. You could fit them on a single piece of paper. Today there is a thick rulebook. We never imagined some of the issues that would require rules. Back in 1973, we just wanted to get a race off the ground and we were feeling our way along.

Joe Redington became known as "Father of the Iditarod."

We proved the skeptics wrong

Raymie Redington and I thought we were a couple of guys who knew what cold was all about. We learned in the first Iditarod race about REAL cold.

Teller and Penny led the way to the Iditarod finish line in 1974.

FOR EVERYONE like Joe Redington who believed in the Iditarod, there were ten doubters in the mushing community who thought it would never happen.

The biggest question, even among those entered, was whether the money would be there to pay the $50,000 purse. George Attla was vocal about it. Some Native mushers were concerned they were going to all this expense to bring their dogs to Anchorage and the payoff wouldn't be there.

To allay the fears, some of us persuaded Bob Fleming, who owned KYAK radio, to write the Iditarod a $50,000 check. He told us that it would bounce like a rubber ball if we tried to cash it, but we had something to show. Even Governor Egan was in on this deal. It was pretty funny. But Egan believed the Iditarod would be good for Alaska and he wanted to see it happen.

Even if the race were planned as a one-time event Egan could see how it would bring notoriety to the state. In the beginning, we couldn't get either the *Anchorage Daily News* or the *Anchorage Times* to show much interest. Then Slim Randles, who worked for the *Daily News*, signed up to race. His wife Pam agreed to follow along (the Iditarod Trail Committee was going to shuttle her) and to send back daily reports. That would give the newspapers something to print.

At a kickoff get-together at the old Gold Rush Hotel in Anchorage, there was a lot of grumbling about the money. It was on everybody's mind. Joe got up and guaranteed there would be a $50,000 purse at the finish line in Nome. Everybody calmed down. We never had to show Fleming's check. Joe had credibility.

Joe had every intention of running the race, but everyone told him he should stay behind to make certain the money was going to be available. Joe felt bad about this, and so did everyone else, but he realized they were right. The most important thing he could do was raise the money.

I had made five hundred plaques with the Iditarod shield on them to mark the trail. A day before the start I nailed some of them up between Tudor Track and Knik. The next day, when the race started, almost every one was gone. People stole them for souvenirs. They were beautiful plaques. So I guess that meant excitement was growing. This created a funny situation. All the mushers had to wait for me to show them the trail out through the Fort Richardson area.

We honestly didn't know if the race would be successful. Would we reach Nome? The Army had gone ahead of us on snowmachines. They left well head of the field and hadn't even gotten to McGrath when the race began. That was only four hundred miles. We weren't sure what to make of this.

We didn't know what to carry in our sleds. We had to be ready for anything. Ron Aldrich had a big tent and a stove. I had a heavy chainsaw. Everyone had large freight sleds. My sled weighed one hundred pounds! If I raced today, my sled would weigh about twenty-five pounds. We were loaded to the hilt. This was more of a camping trip than a race. We all knew there was a big prize at the end, but we didn't know how much actual racing we would be able to do.

There was a tremendous crowd for the March 3, 1973 start. The sight at the starting line was impressive. Nobody had ever seen thirty-odd teams hooked up to freight sleds. We knew this was something big. We just didn't know exactly what.

Some mushers had big names and reputations as smart dog men. George Attla, Herbie Nayokpuk, Isaac Okleasik, John Komak, and Bobby Vent had been racing dogs for years in the villages and seemed to know what they were doing.

Those of us who were more urban cowboys thought all this was pretty cool. I had no notion I could win the race. Most of us saw it as a grand adventure and just wanted to get to Nome. Later, once we realized we could get there, we started thinking competitively.

Mostly we traveled in groups. If you came to a place at five or six o'clock at night and it was getting dark, you made camp. Why go any farther? Everyone else piled into camp right behind you. And you left in groups about seven o'clock the next morning. That's the way most of the race went.

The comraderie was great. We built bonfires and sat around BSing. We talked about dogs and the trail and what we were doing. Two or three days into it, we realized what we were up against—the distance and the weather.

Bobby Vent and I were running together when we got to Susitna Station. We got horribly tangled up in some willows. We went ten feet and pieces of willow got stuck through our sled stanchions. We had to take an axe and cut ourselves free. Then we'd go another ten feet and get hung up again. I started laughing and Bobby said, "I don't see anything funny about it." I said, "I do. Howard Farley's behind us with a sixteen-foot coastal freight sled." It was two feet wide. Farley was going to have to come through the same mess. It took him hours to cut through.

When we got to Happy River, we found out the Army snowmachines had gone up the river instead of on the trail. We were going along a cliff on a semblance of trail on shelf ice. Don Sheldon landed his Super Cub on a ridge above us and hollered, "What are you doing down there? The trail is up here." The old Iditarod Trail was above the river, but until then no one had found it.

I was traveling with Ron Aldrich and Raymie Redington. As we started down the ice of the Happy River, the trail made a ninety-degree turn left to the precipice of a ravine, and we went flying out over it and into the ravine one right on top of another. What a mess. We spent two hours getting out of that tangle and back up onto the trail.

We didn't gripe about it, though. Our attitude was more, "Wow, what a deal!" These days the world would come to an end if you had to contend with something like that on the Iditarod Trail, which the frontrunners are trying to finish in nine days. But in 1973, we felt our way along. When we reached Puntilla Lake at the Rainy Pass Lodge, we thought we had accomplished something.

Actually, most of the trail had been good and so was the weather. I camped with Aldrich, Raymie Redington, Ron Oviak, and John Komak. We might be separated for a day, depending on our pace, then get back together. We were the second group, though. The leaders were ahead of us.

When I got to McGrath, there was Dick Tozier, the race marshal. He said, "You know, you're averaging the same speed as the lead bunch, about five-and-one-half miles an hour." Turns out the leaders were running more hours each day. I made up my mind that I was going to catch up, and maybe be a contender, because the dogs were doing great.

Then I ran into a huge snowstorm. We're talking major snow, about two feet of it. Ron Oviak had never been on a pair of snowshoes in his life, so Ron Aldrich and I did most of the trail-breaking. It took us nine hours to go seventeen miles. Basically, Ron and I were the lead dogs.

At Big River, between Nikolai and McGrath, Joe had stationed a checker. He was living in a pup tent and hardly knew where he was. He had a radio and called in the names and times as you passed by. Nearby was a beaver trapper from Nikolai who had just moved into his spring trapping cabin. Esau Esau was his name. He and his wife invited four of us into his cabin for the night.

After breakfast the next morning, we were anxious to leave. The checker spread the word to Tozier in McGrath that there was no trail ahead and told us that snowmachines were on the way. Esau volunteered to be our trailbreaker. We weren't expecting much speed. The whole previous day we'd led the teams on snowshoes, moving so slowly the dogs stepped on the back of our feet.

Esau put on the snowshoes, got into a running shuffle, and for the next five miles—in two feet of snow, mind you—never stopped. *He didn't stop for five miles!* We were floundering with our heavy loads trying to keep up. It was the most awesome display of snowshoeing I'd ever seen. He led us to a portage across a river, and then stepped to the side. I can remember turning around and there he went, shuffling back in the direction he had come, moving just as fast. I never forgot that. Years later I saw Esau again and reminded him of how fast he moved that day. He just smiled.

After the storm played out and the wind died, bitter cold set in. I was having a ball, despite the frustrations and hard work. At times it was 30 below zero. We didn't have adequate clothing. This was before mushers wore layered clothing. Our approach was to put on everything you had—wool on wool on wool. It was all wrong.

I enjoyed learning from some of these older Bush mushers. During a cold spell I traveled with John Komak and he invited me to make camp with him. He told me to bring my food and sleeping bag. Using a snow-shoe, he dug into the snow about two and one-half feet at the edge of the trail. Then he draped one end of a piece of parachute over the handlebar of his sled and the other over a snowshoe stuck in the snow. John made a tent over the trench he had dug. Then he pulled out his Coleman stove and put it down into the trench. We sat with our backs against the sled. The heat was below us, keeping us toasty warm. I was impressed. Most people would have just set the stove onto the trail and much of the heat would have been wasted.

It was snowing hard when I left McGrath. It let up some, and then it snowed some more. I was traveling alone and saw a village in the distance. It was Takotna. The trail swung to the left, but if you went maybe a half-mile too far to the right you ended up in Takotna. It was noontime, and I thought I could use a cup of coffee or some hot soup.

A guy who introduced himself as Dave was waving his arms as I ap-proached the village. He told me I had missed the trail. I told him I knew I was off it, but wanted something hot to drink. He said there was no cafe but invited me into his home.

When I got ready to leave, Dave, who owned a bar, gave me a bottle of whiskey. I put it in a wool sock and tucked it into my sled bag. Then I hit the trail, and soon the snow stopped and the temperature dropped. It got down to about 60 below. I was cold and tired, and things weren't going well. Even with my backcountry experience, 60 below was cold—a terrible penetrating cold. And it had been a hard day. It didn't seem as if I was going to reach Ophir, the next checkpoint.

So I set up camp. I put a tarp over my sled, started my stove, and sat in the sled. Raymie Redington mushed up and parked his team, and then he ducked under the tarp with me. "Man, I've never been so cold in my life," he said.

We thought we were a couple of guys who knew what cold was all about. We learned then, and in subsequent years on the Iditarod, about *real* cold. I remembered having the booze and pulled the bottle out of the sock. The whiskey was slush. Now that's cold.

We stayed huddled together next to the trail for six or seven hours. We fed the dogs, we made tea, and we shivered. Finally, we couldn't sit still any longer, and off we went. No more than fifteen minutes later we bumped into Ron Aldrich and Tom Mercer's dog teams sitting in front of a cabin. What the hey?

Aldrich told us the cabin belonged to a woman in the Pioneer Home in Palmer who had given him permission to use it. Another five minutes down the trail was the cabin of Dick and Audra Forsgren, who had hung a lantern out for us. So there were two cabins within twenty minutes from where we sat freezing on the trail for hours. The Forsgrens were feeding everybody. It was great. But we had spent a horrible night out for no reason.

The Iditarod Trail has a lot of history. That first year we felt a sense of discovery. It was old territory, but it felt like new territory. We were soaking it up.

At Poorman, pieces and parts of an old roadhouse still stood. It had been an elaborate place in its heyday. There were huge old steam engines out there, too, left over from mining in the early part of the last century. We ran into people who knew the country. I wondered how the heck the steam engines had been brought in. Howard Miskovitch, who lived on a mining claim with his wife, Donna, told me it had taken a couple of years to get the engines to the site. First, an engine was brought to Seattle, then carried to St. Michael by boat, and floated by barge to Ruby on the Yukon River. Finally, using twenty oxen, the miners hauled in an engine to where it sits today. Then they ate the oxen. A year later they repeated the process, bringing in a second steam engine.

Today we've got to do everything in such a hurry. These guys spent years bringing in two steam engines. They needed them to thaw the ground so they could put their shafts down. All this intrigued me.

After the race, I got a call from Joe. He said Howard Miskovitch was upset. The dogs had polluted the snow they used for drinking water, and some of the mushers left trash around. Joe and I flew out there, cleaned the place up, and made amends.

I caught up with Herbie and Isaac in Ruby. That night I got leg cramps and thought I would push the logs out of the wall in Kelly Painter's cabin. Then, when I mushed on to Galena, I caught the flu. I felt lousy.

In Galena, I ran into Terry Adkins, who later ran the Iditarod more than twenty times. He was the only vet on hand for the first race. Sidney Huntington, the well-respected elder from Galena, opened his home for use as a checkpoint, and we were staying there. Terry was Mr. Fix-it with the dogs, and he compared me catching the flu to "kennel cough" running through a dog team. There were a fair number of people around and little privacy, but he got me off to the side, I pulled down my pants, and he gave me a shot in the butt. I have no idea what the stuff was, but it worked. A day later I was feeling better.

Then I found out that George Attla was holed up in a cabin there with his dog team *inside*. The dogs weren't feeling too well. I felt good about catching up to George Attla.

On the way from Galena to Koyukuk, we ran into warm weather, and Herbie Nayokpuk and I stopped to make some tea. Just pulling over was no big deal in the early days of the Iditarod. I was hot and had too many clothes on. When Herbie peeled off his parka, all he had on was a T-shirt. That's what he'd had on at 60 below. I said, "Herbie, is that all you're wearing?" He laughed and said, "Usually, I don't wear a T-shirt, but when you go into some white guy's house, he expects you to have something on."

Herbie and I took off together and mushed into Koyukuk. The village wasn't a checkpoint, but as we mushed along the villagers were hollering to us from a bank. "Hey, come on up!" they said. The people who lived on the trail were one hundred percent into the race. We didn't know when we left Anchorage that we would be greeted so warmly. Everybody made you feel good. You'd run into someone who knew who you were, or they knew somebody you knew. They fed you, put you up, and you went on your way. In 1973, there were still quite a few dog teams in the villages. The people identified with us.

There was more history in Kaltag, where we saw a wire strung through the trees. I thought, "What the heck is that?" Turned out to be part of the old Russian-American telegraph line.

By then I was moving right along. I was *racing*. I wasn't near the front, but I seemed to be moving up. Then, leaving Unalakleet, heading for Shaktoolik, we got hit by another bad snowstorm. We sat in Shaktoolik for twenty-eight hours. I was with Herbie Nayokpuk and along came Attla.

Herbie joked, "Boy, I'm sure glad to be out of Indian country." The Eskimos, who lived on the tundra near the coast, had dogs that had never run in timber found inland. When the wind blew, the trees shook, and the dogs were spooked.

Attla, who is Athabascan, laughed at the weather and said, "I don't know if I'm going to like this Eskimo country or not."

This was a storm so fierce not even the coastal Eskimos would go out into it. So nobody went. When it abated somewhat, Herbie and Isaac Okleasik decided they would go for it. They took out some rabbit pelts and tied them around the mid-section of the male dogs, so the dogs wouldn't freeze their, uh, *deal*. We had never seen anything like that before, so we urban cowboys cut some Army blankets into strips and did the same thing. And off we went.

We made it to Elim and needed some rest. While John Komak and I slept, Herbie and Issac quietly slipped away.

We were getting close to Nome, and I'm starting to think this was going to be a race after all. Komak and I were together. We came into White Mountain together, went on to Topkok, and headed for Solomon. It was a beautiful, sunny day, and we were starting to wear down the dogs. We were starting to wear down, too.

Finally, we approached Nome. I wanted to beat John, but I felt funny about it. At the start, mushers had left at two-minute intervals. They still do. Because of our starting positions, I could come in twenty minutes behind John and still beat him. It didn't seem right. In those days the times weren't adjusted along the trail with mandatory rests to put everybody on an equal footing at the end of the race. But I knew then there was no way John Komak was going to accept that I had finished behind him and still beat him.

So I had to get ahead of him. In the final miles I picked up the pace. Let me tell you, I never worked so hard to get ahead of somebody in my life. Suddenly, we were both mushing faster. And he's a tough guy. I had a lot of respect for him. This had nothing to do with a few dollars more in prize money. I got him. Later, when the starting times had been factored in, officially I beat John by thirty-three minutes for seventh place after a little more than twenty-one days on the trail.

Dick Wilmarth won the race in just over twenty days. Bobby Vent took second, Dan Seavey third, and Attla fourth. Herbie and Isaac finished ahead of me.

Just getting there was great. We basked in the feeling.

We were part of something special. That's one reason why, no matter how tired we were or what we were doing, we rushed to the finish line with just about the entire population of Nome when we heard the siren blaring announcing that another musher was coming down Front Street. We all went out to greet him. No one was left out.

This went on for days.

I finished seventh in the first Iditarod race in 1973.

"Mighty men, these dog drivers"

I developed a special bond with other mushers who ran the first Iditarod. I might not see them often, but they are always friends. We are part of a brotherhood.

Moments after crossing the finish line in 1974.
©Richard Burmeister/Alaska Stock Images

TWENTY-TWO MUSHERS drove teams about eleven hundred miles across Alaska that first year. The early finishers gathered in Nome for the awards presentation, a modest version of what grew into a huge annual banquet that attracts more than one thousand people. But back in 1973, we met in the basement of the old Northern Commercial Co. store.

I don't recall that a meal was served but lo and behold we all got a check. Not everybody kept theirs. Dan Seavey of Seward, who placed third, donated his $6,000 back to the race. It was an impressive gesture. More than twenty-five years later, Dan's son Mitch is an Iditarod contender, and his grandson Danny is racing too. All three generations entered the 2001 Iditarod. That's got the Mackeys beat.

At the awards ceremony, Joe Redington shouted out, "Well, should we have another race next year?" Everybody cheered and hollered, and that was the first time anybody talked about running another race to Nome.

Dorothy Page wanted to open up the Iditarod Trail. Joe Redington wanted preserve sled dogs and mushing. They both got what they wanted.

The Iditarod became a way of life for me as the race quickly shifted from a one-time adventure to a permanent fixture. From the beginning, the Iditarod changed the public perception of the value of dogs, the importance of dogs in the wilderness, and increased the stature of the Alaska husky. Joe Redington always said the dogs could do just about everything, and he was right.

Even before we reached Nome the dogs and mushers had made an impression on Alaskans. When I reached Golovin, about one-thousand miles from Anchorage, all the villagers were lined up to watch. Everybody was dressed in their finery, especially the women, who put on their fancy parkas each time a team came in.

I can remember one woman holding the hand of a little girl, both watching as I mushed in with another driver. She said, "Mighty men, these dog drivers." What a comment! It made us stand up a little straighter.

If you looked into the eyes of the older men, you could see they were dreaming. They wanted to be on the trail, too. The villagers got solidly behind the race in the years to come, whether working on the trail or volunteering at a checkpoint. Yet at times the Iditarod failed them miserably. Didn't even say thank you. We promised them gasoline and parts for their snowmachines and didn't come through. In part this was because the Iditarod was such a small operation in the beginning, just a handful of people compared to the larger, more formal organization it is today. And in part it was because of money. We didn't have any. Whoever was around worked so hard to put the race on that details were overlooked.

I was surprised at the reaction of the public. Nome was the only place I knew of you could walk down the street with a can of beer in each hand and a cop would say, "You having a good time?" The Iditarod finishers were royalty in Nome.

And when I got home to Wasilla, same thing. The Iditarod race went overnight from a quirky idea to an event everyone wanted to be part of.

Dick Wilmarth was a quiet guy, a miner from Sleetmute, who didn't go out and promote himself as winner of the first Iditarod. You never saw him with endorsement contracts such as the top mushers have today. In fact, Wilmarth never ran the race again. But it didn't matter. That first year we were all winners. The guy who crossed the finish line last—John Schultz—was as much a winner as Wilmarth, except Wilmarth earned more prize money.

A musher named Tom Mercer placed eighteenth and was on the trail for more than thirty-one days. He lost eighty-one pounds out there! Tom had been a hospital administrator in the East who finally threw up his hands and said, "The heck with this lifestyle," and moved to Alaska.

With the winners now finishing the Iditarod in about nine days, it is incomprehensible that some of the first mushers spent more than a month on the trail.

In 1975, a guy named Steve Fee took the red lantern for last place. He was twenty-fifth and last. When you hear the term "running" the Iditarod it usually means guiding the dogs to Nome. But in Steve's case, he covered the last ninety miles from White Mountain on snowshoes. There wasn't any trail left, and Steve was the only musher who had not finished. He and his team got to Nome six days behind the next-to-last musher. But he made it.

In 1973, finishing was the most important thing. This is still true today, even as the Iditarod approaches its thirtieth year with more prize money and faster dogs.

Later, when I served on the Iditarod Trail Committee, I developed the theory that essentially there were three groups within the race. You had the true contenders, the wannabes, and those who simply wanted to finish, whether year after year or just once. It was the middle group that caused all the problems. The wannabes complained about the weather, the trail, or the rules. The committee was bad; everything was to blame except the wannabe's own incompetence.

Even though the spirit of the Iditarod endures and the other early Iditarod runs were similar, you can't duplicate the feeling of the first year. Those in that race were the pioneers, and a large number of them never raced again, or competed just once more. Now we have people who race every year. My son Rick has been a regular since 1975.

A lot of the first-year racers were attracted to the Iditarod because it was something new and different and it offered the thrill of going into the unknown. Once it was shown the Iditarod could be done, and they had done it, maybe it lost its allure for them.

Everyone who ran in 1973 received a patch that said, "Iditarod Trailblazer." Each subsequent year you ran they gave you a little chevron with the date on it. They've done away with those over the years. The patches were replaced by the finisher's belt buckle.

I developed a special connection with those mushers who participated in the first Iditarod. I might see some of them a couple of times a year, but they were friends. We were all part of a brotherhood.

Howard Farley and I fished together in Nome that first year. I had good friendships with Tom Mercer and Ron Aldrich. George Attla and I were always good friends. I saw Dick Wilmarth, Bobby Vent or Bill Arpino a few times a year.

I ran into Dan Seavey before the start of the 2000 Iditarod for the first time in a while and we greeted each other warmly. There was a bond because of what we shared twenty-seven years earlier.

After the first year, many ideas were floated about the route. Someone suggested we start in Seward, 120 miles from Anchorage, and run the entire Iditarod Trail.

Even after the publicity and the success of the first Iditarod, I had problems getting permits for a second year. The state highway department didn't want us to hold up traffic between Anchorage and Knik while the dogs crossed the bridges on the Matanuska Flats.

We ran alongside the Glenn Highway, and there was always the possibility the dogs would run out onto the road. By the third year, we developed a plan for mushers to leave downtown Anchorage and run only to Eagle River before loading the dogs in trucks to be taken to Wasilla for a re-start.

Some years we re-started in Wasilla, close to Iditarod headquarters. Other times we started at Nancy Lake, or Settler's Bay, wherever there was enough snow. The lack of consistently good snow in Southcentral Alaska put the kibosh on the idea of running in reverse, from Nome to Anchorage. And it wasn't like we could finish in tiny Knik. Where would we put the crowds? There was talk of finishing at the Alaska State Fairgrounds in Palmer. People were looking at new ideas. But it stayed the way it began, a race from Anchorage to Nome. I don't think it's going to change now.

The only major course change was addition of a southern route for the odd years, starting in 1977. That way, the Iditarod runs through more villages, involves more people, and gives trailbreakers a break. It's worked out well.

The Iditarod has been successful in so many ways. It was successful because we made it to the finish line. It was successful because it became popular. It was successful because it put the spotlight on Alaska huskies. It was successful because we got U.S. Senator Mike Gravel to sponsor federal legislation designating the Iditarod Trail a National Historic Trail. And it was successful because the Iditarod added immeasurably to nutrition and care of dogs.

We lost too many dogs in the first few years. It was not because we didn't care or that we mistreated them, or because we weren't trying. It was because of ignorance. Over the years, though, mushers and veterinarians learned together by cooperating, and the level of care has become phenomenal. The dogs love to run. They love it. Everyone has to understand that. The dogs are checked constantly along the trail now.

There have been so many advancements. This is equally true of the equipment. Everything now is lighter and more sophisticated and high tech. In 1973 we were using old-time gear in an old-time sport. People had steel runners on their sleds. Now mushers run on plastic runners.

Tim White from Minnesota, who became a famous sled maker, raced the Iditarod in 1974 and introduced new-fangled, smaller sleds. His equipment was the gear of the future.

One thing I learned quickly was that the best Iditarod dog I had was the worst sprint dog. You needed a dog who had cast-iron feet, who ate like there was no tomorrow, who would sleep on command, and who could trot.

My first four years in the Iditarod I had a leader named Penny. By the third year she was so savvy you could crawl into the sled and go to sleep and she would never leave the trail. By the fourth year Penny was still going to go to Nome, but she was going to go at her own pace. If she'd gone over a cliff, I swear she'd have done it slowly.

A good leader is remarkable. There was a place on the trail between Skwentna and Finger Lake where there was a little cluster of trees. For three years it was easier to go to the *right* of the trees. I came along the fourth year and there was drifted snow. It would have been easier to go to the *left*, but Penny never hesitated. She jumped out into the deep snow to go to the right of the trees where the trail had always been.

For the first three years of the race I stayed at the home of Norm and Marylou Stiles in Unalakleet. We mushed through the village to their house. The fourth year we ran up the slough behind the village, coming from a different direction. Penny led the team right up to the house and lay down in the same spot where she'd been before. She had never been that way. That's how good those dogs are. She was a great dog.

Penny's mother Betsy was the first dog I ever bred and raced. Betsy was thirteen years old when I retired her from the Iditarod. When she was seventeen, she had a litter of pups. Betsy weaned those puppies and then died from natural causes. Within the hour Penny died of natural causes.

Mushers develop a special bond with their dogs after spending so much time together on the trail. The dogs are like family. And you miss them when they are gone.

Keeping the Iditarod alive

*I dug some dental floss from my bag, tied one
end to the sled, and set out into the fierce storm
holding the other. That's how I found the trail.*

Taking care of business on the Iditarod Trail.
©Jim Brown/Alaska Stock Images

ORGANIZING the second Iditarod took almost as much effort as making the first one happen. We had all kinds of meetings with mushers who lived in the Knik, Wasilla, and Anchorage areas. Once the excitement of success wore off, we realized shortcomings needed to be corrected.

For one thing, we had a terrible time getting dropped dogs back to Nome or Anchorage. We didn't have enough planes. It was a disaster getting the dogs to the right places. We were in an evolutionary stage.

In other ways, once we had done it, the race was easier to put on. People knew who we were. One thing I did between the 1973 and 1974 races was to go to every checkpoint, flying with Jim Christopher. I went to someone in every village and told them what we expected from checkers.

Of course, we were in debt over our heads. We managed to survive because we conned everybody into giving us what we needed. Some were donations. Some stuff we never paid for. We were always a dollar short.

I never understood why we couldn't raise more money. Alaska was in a boom period. The trans-Alaska Pipeline was being built to bring the oil from Prudhoe Bay to Valdez. The economy was good. And we didn't waste money. I was on the Iditarod board of directors for thirteen years, so I was close to it, and I can tell you we were always short of money.

We held board meetings all over the place. I never missed a board meeting in thirteen years and I never received any remuneration. Nobody got paid for anything. You knew you weren't going to be reimbursed. The pilots didn't get fed. Sometimes they got gasoline. The snowmachiners who were the trailbreakers might get a spare part. We had growing pains.

In the second Iditarod, we had a different group of mushers. But I knew I was going to be back and stay with it. I never had any doubt. It was a good fit for me. By the second race I figured I could be a contender, though I didn't go into it thinking I would win.

In the first three Iditarods, I was thinking more about helping the race stay alive than I was thinking about how well I could finish. I understood that with my organizational duties I didn't have enough time to train.

In 1974, I ran all of the way up the trail to Galena with Carl Huntington. Carl was a great sprint musher. He won that year. Native mushers were the frontrunners then. This showed how the villages embraced the Iditarod. The Eskimo and Indian mushers were expert dog men. They lived with their dogs, worked with their dogs, depended on them in their subsistence lifestyle. Now the Iditarod has become a 365-day-a-year job for the top competitors. Most of the Native mushers don't have the financing to stay up there among the frontrunners. Their lifestyles interfere. They fish. They hunt. They are in remote Bush communities, where it is harder to get sponsorship.

It was a big thing in the Bush when Carl won. Emmitt Peters of Ruby, "The Yukon Fox," won the race the next year. Then Jerry Riley of Nenana won. Native mushers were winning every year.

I placed tenth in the 1974 Iditarod. My training was not helped by the double hernia I had the preceding November. I went to the family doctor for something minor. I remember he was writing out a prescription and he said, "How long has it been since you had a physical?" It had been a long time. He said he thought I should have one, and I said I would make an appointment. He said, "No, right now."

So I had a physical. He looked me over and said, "You know, it's a wonder you don't fall apart picking up a coffee cup. You've got one of the worst hernias I've ever seen." A few hours later I was on the operating table, being cut open by a different doctor.

Afterward I had all this stainless steel mesh in my abdomen. I was a complainer. I had a dog team to train. He told me if I listened to his advice I'd be able to train in six weeks.

The guy in the bed next to me had a hernia operation and went home the next day. They told me I had to stay a week. When I asked why he got to go home so fast, of course they told me it was because I had a double hernia. I figured a double hernia was only worth two days.

Finally, the doctor said, "When you can walk down that hallway and back, you can go home." Two days later, I left. I walked to the end of the hallway, but I thought it would kill me. I doubled over. I had to keep coming back for checkups and sure enough the last one was six weeks later. I was happy and said, "Well, today's the day." The doctor gave me a go-ahead to run dogs. By then it was the first part of January.

I rushed home and hooked up fourteen dogs and went off on the first training run since the operation. As soon as I left the dog yard I knew I had made a mistake. I was bouncing up and down on the sled and was yanking and pulling as I held the handlebars. I took the shortest run I could, about five miles.

I came back into the dog yard yelling, "Get me to the doctor!" The kids unhooked the team, and we headed into Anchorage. I got into the doctor's office all doubled over and holding my stomach as if I was holding my innards in. He said, "What's the matter?" I said I was coming apart. He actually laughed.

"I said you could run dogs," he said. "I didn't say it wasn't going to hurt."

He said I would be fine soon enough if I could put up with it. I had a painful training season and a painful Iditarod, too. The operation took a lot out of me, and I never should have run that year. Finishing tenth was pretty good, but all in all it was a bad year.

It was a tough year on the trail. There was a bad storm in Rainy Pass. Five of us spent the night in a group. Joe Redington was an hour behind and spent the night out alone. I think I was with Carl Huntington, Warner Vent, Dan Seavey, and Jerry Riley. We hunkered down in what was the worst storm we'd ever been in.

It was cold and blowing. We didn't even have a bush to get behind. We put all of the dogs together, climbed into our sleeping bags for warmth, and made sure we all stayed awake. From time to time we checked on each other, all night long. Afterward, we found out that the wind-chill factor had been

130 degrees below zero. We wore better clothing than we'd had the year before, but it wasn't warm enough.

I'm not sure there's anything warm enough in those circumstances. The best clothing keeps you from freezing, but you're not comfortable. Eddie Bauer used to put out a catalogue that included a sleeping bag they said was rated to minus 70. They sponsored my son Rick one year, gave him everything—beautiful stuff. All of their marketing people came to Nome, vice presidents and all.

Then they brought Rick to Seattle. They wanted him to evaluate all the gear. Poor Rick. He thought they wanted the truth. He told them that whoever comfort-rated the bag to minus 70 was nuts. That was the only year Eddie Bauer sponsored him.

The fact is, when the wind chill gets as cold as minus 130, you're just trying to survive it. Never mind comfort. Victor Katonga's mother made him some caribou hide sleeping bags. They must have weighed twenty-five pounds apiece. I don't know of anything else that works when it's that cold.

In the 1970s, I got a test sleeping bag from Paul Petzoldt at the National Outdoor Leadership School, made it in conjunction with Dupont. They also gave me a parka and mitts that were excellent. The sleeping bag was adequate, but in the worst cases it offered little comfort. Grade it a B+. It was an experimental bag. The second year they provided me with another sleeping bag. This one you could put in the washing machine.

I spent one night out in the sleeping bag in a ground storm between Shaktoolik and Koyuk. The next morning, I couldn't get out of the bag. The zipper was frozen shut. I pulled out my knife inside the bag and unceremoniously slit it open to get out.

The leadership school brought me to Lander, Wyoming for a presentation, but they were horrified by the Iditarod stories I told them. This was an ultraconservative group. They couldn't identify with the race. They didn't believe in using toilet paper in the wild. To them, the only time you built a campfire was in a life-threatening situation—for the heat, not for sitting around and telling stories.

The night we all camped together to wait out that minus-130 windchill was fearsome. There was no shelter. If the snow had been deeper we could have made a snow shelter, but it was wind-blown country. We stopped because we had reached a point where it would have been too dangerous to continue. Not that it was safe to remain still. But we had no other options. We had to do one or the other. This was the only time I ever felt I was in a life-threatening situation.

The storm ended in the morning, and the sun came out. But there was no trail. We had to get going and get on to Rohn for more dog food. We were moving but we weren't racing. It wasn't until later that Carl pulled away, and the places sorted themselves out.

The Iditarod is a hard race and it can be hard on your body. Sometimes mushers are doing so many last-minute things, they don't even come well rested to the start. In 1974, Bobby Vent was sixty-three, and he had to scratch because of pneumonia. He didn't go far. There's a lot of stress. Some people get the flu right before the race.

In 1980, I scratched in Unalakleet and had to go to the hospital. I was in bad shape. I had ruptured my stomach and was bleeding internally. By the time I found out what was wrong, I had nearly died.

The first few years, the Iditarod race committee was concerned that someone might die on the trail. It was conceivable and sometimes seemed *probable*. We were afraid if anyone died, there would be an outcry that would end the race.

There are any number of ways someone could die in the race. It could be as simple as an apparently healthy athlete having a heart attack. Age doesn't enter into it. When people think about someone dying in the Iditarod, mostly they fear someone being caught out in a storm and being separated from their team.

And accidents can happen. We've had broken arms, broken legs, illnesses. It's so easy for a musher to bang his head against a tree, hitting a low-hanging branch after falling asleep on the sled. It's all happened.

One of the scariest moments I ever had occurred in the 1976 race. That was the first year I thought I had a chance to win. I was leading when I left Unalakleet on the Bering Sea Coast. I was seven-and-one-half-hours ahead and thinking, "I'm going to win this race."

A storm was coming, but I was determined to beat it. I left Unalakleet after dark and before long I had a sense we had gotten off the trail. I set the hook and was down on hands and knees feeling the ground. By then the storm had hit. I put on my headlamp and took half a dozen steps to the left. No trail. When I turned around *my team was gone*. But I suspected the dogs hadn't moved—I was just looking in the wrong place.

Blinded by fierce wind and snow, forcing myself to stay calm, I walked in a widening circle. My heart was pounding. Several minutes passed. Then I tripped over a dog. I'd found the team! I dug into my bag and found some dental floss. I tied the floss to the sled handle and set out again holding tightly to the other end. That's how I found the trail.

Picking up the pace

For a dreamer, the Iditarod promises adventure.
He can't become an astronaut, but he can run the
Iditarod, if he is tough and has the will to do it.

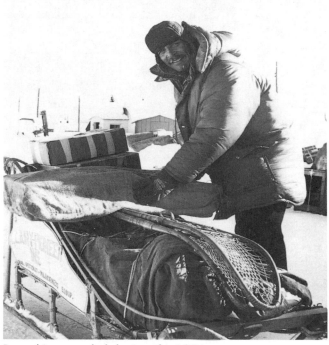

Repacking my sled during the 1974 race.
©Anchorage Museum of History & Art/Alaska Stock Images

THE 1974 RACE was hard for me. There were times out there when I thought if a helicopter had come along and offered to pluck me off the trail, I would have been willing. But I've never been one to turn back. I've always thought it was just as easy to go ahead to the next checkpoint as it was to turn back to the last one.

I'm of the mind if you can move at all, you move. Psychologically, when you get to the checkpoint, you feel as if you've done something. You might feel better, and it might keep you going. If you think you're going to scratch, you're in no hurry when you get to a checkpoint. You have time to think about it.

Early in his Iditarod career, Joe Redington made the mistake of mushing into a checkpoint and immediately scratching from the race. Then he went to sleep. In the morning he felt better, his dogs looked better, and he was sorry he was out of the race. So his advice became: Sleep on it. It may be that the dogs will have a good long rest and eat well. Then they stand up and look pretty good, and you think, "Hey!"

Some people who run the Iditarod have negative thoughts. They're just who they are. There always will be setbacks. I try to look ahead. My parents never looked back. Surely that has something to do with my outlook.

Funny thing is, though I've always lived in a cold climate, I get cold easily. Most of the time I've worn enough clothing so it doesn't make any difference how cold it gets. I was plenty cold in that huge storm out of Unalakleet. After the storm passed, getting to the next checkpoint became an ordeal for everybody because their dogs were weakened. We kept thinking we would be fine if we survived the night.

One of the things a fan might not recognize from a distance is how much of a team a musher and his dogs are. You take five guys on a basketball team. They come out on the court and they're a cohesive unit. Football, baseball, it doesn't make any difference. Any team effort. They communicate. Now, take a dog team of sixteen animals and you can't communicate with them, but through repetition you work them into a cohesive team. It's a hell of an accomplishment. That's what it's all about. I've got sixteen dogs, you've got sixteen dogs, and I believe we're a better team than you are. Now we're going see if I'm right, if we can do it as a team. That's the uniqueness of the Iditarod.

Because it's such a long race, there are many factors—the health of the dogs, the health of the musher, trail conditions, weather.

What makes the Iditarod so appealing to the average lay person is the adventure. They're awed by it. Joe Schmo is sitting in an office gazing out the window on a sunny day and wonders how his life ever got to the point where he sits at a desk all day. He's wondering what else he could do. He knows he can't become an astronaut and go to the moon. But he can run the Iditarod, if he has the will and the toughness. Don Montgomery of Lima, Ohio was an insurance man. He completed the Iditarod in 1979. It was the greatest achievement of his life. People relate to that.

Some people start with three-dog or five-dog teams in sprint races. Most of them are kids. I always thought that was perfect for juniors. But I ridiculed adults who wanted to run a three-dog team. First thing you knew, they would want trophies, then prize money.

However, I changed my mind. After a while I saw nothing wrong with starting this way. What I question is, why have the same three-dog team year after year? Why not try to get better? It's the same with the Iditarod. Do it once for the adventure, but keep improving. If not, the musher is on an adventure, not in a race. It's wonderful to fantasize about doing it once. Come one and all! There's nothing wrong with being dead last. But the next year they should be a little better, not just in putting together a team, but in the whole operation—dog care, nutrition, knowledge.

People who are content to stand still irritate me. I feel the same way about people in every profession. If you're going to be a writer, always try to improve your work. If you're a carpenter, try to be the best you can be.

Placing tenth in 1974 earned me $573. Hoo boy. What was that, a penny an hour? That didn't even pay for gas. But I wasn't thinking about money. I finished seventh in 1975, and it felt like a lost year. Everything was faster. We had better weather. The race, which had been taking three weeks, was finished in two weeks.

This was a big change. The Iditarod went from being a camping trip to finding out what some of the competitors had learned. We had better nutrition, better vet care. No longer were we running purely sprint dogs. Now you knew what you needed. A good dog today is identical to a good dog in 1973. The only thing is, back then I had one of them and now I would have a whole team of them. The trail was adequate then, now it's a boulevard by comparison. The 1975 race was the beginning of all that. We stretched out the racing day. Instead of running from seven to five during the day, mushers were going all night.

Emmitt Peters had a great run. He was fast and aggressive. He went all the way home to Ruby, more than six hundred miles, before he took a twenty-four-hour mandatory rest. No one had ever gone that far. Emmitt challenged the boundaries of speed and everyone followed along keeping up a faster pace. Because he was so popular in the Bush, he had people trailing him on snowmachines and cooking his food while he slept. This was perfectly legal at the time. Later, the rules were changed to prohibit outside assistance.

The rulebook got fatter—and more technical—as time passed. Now you almost need an attorney to interpret it. New rules evolved from incidents along the trail that raised questions no one had anticipated.

My son Rick, then twenty-two, ran his first race in 1975. He finished thirteenth. I was elated when Rick signed up. He had been active in mushing since he was a little kid. We worked together on the trail. We had trained some together. I was tickled when he got back into dogs after taking a couple of years off. The whole family was excited about it.

At the time it was hard to visualize he would become a champion. Of course, after I won everyone called him "Dick's son" for a few years. Now when I drive into Fairbanks, and somebody at a store hears my name, they say, "Mackey, like the musher? You must be Rick's father." This suits me just fine. Rick is the only musher ever to win the Iditarod and then move over and win the Yukon Quest International Sled Dog Race, a 1,000-mile race between Fairbanks, Alaska, and Whitehorse, Yukon Territory.

There was pressure on Rick after I won in 1978 because he was my son. The next year he took essentially the same dogs on the trail. The dogs were sick by the time he got to McGrath. He finished eighth, and this was considered a failure.

Another son, Bill, did the Iditarod in 1984. He's always had dogs, but he hasn't always wanted to race. Bill's always got the most enjoyment out of camping on the trail, even if only five miles from home. He grew up doing all the junior races and he ran intermediate length events. He got enthused about the Iditarod in 1984 the year after Rick won. Bill came in last, got the red lantern, but his finish was amazing because he was forced to drop all his leaders by the time he reached Ophir.

My third son, Lance, completed his rookie Iditarod in March 2001. Two weeks later he was operated on for cancer. Tough, determined, and fighting mad, he signed up for the 2002 Iditarod. Our family and hundreds of the extended Iditarod family pray daily for his recovery.

Daughter Becky grew up competing in the junior races. As an adult, she ran in several mid-distance races and assisted brother Bill in his sled dog tour business in the Brooks Range.

Youngest son Jason also grew up in the dog lot. He competed in several junior Iditarod races and today runs mid-distance with an eye on the Iditarod and the Yukon Quest.

They've all had dogs. Daughter Kristin entered the picture at Coldfoot about twenty years ago. She was seven when Cathy and I married. She jumped right into the dog life and helped me train. She ran a couple of rinky-dink races up north above the Arctic Circle in Coldfoot and Wiseman and then got out of dogs. Fifty-below weather wasn't her cup of tea at all.

Brenda, Rick's daughter, ran the Yukon Quest. Many of my grandchildren run dogs. Bill's kids mush in the Bettles area. Isaac, Bridget, Rebecca, and Eno give tour rides. Lance has two daughters with dogs. They're all Mackeys. That's a lot of Mackeys with dogs. Jason's got two young sons and eventually they'll get into dogs.

This makes me proud, but I worry, too. It wasn't until I got out of dogs that I started to put a few dollars into my pocket. The average dog musher leads a Spartan life. I look at some of the kids—the older, adult ones—and I shake my head. I drop hints like, "Well, you're not a kid anymore." I say that to get them thinking about the future. They look me square in the eye and say, "I'm not doing anything different than what you did, dad."

It's a lifestyle that's chosen. It's not one that will make you rich. You can make a living with sponsorships, endorsements, breeding and selling dogs, and earning prize money, but you've got to keep producing.

One of the new opportunities in recent years has been the growth of winter tourism. Some visitors want to be guided on long trips into the wilderness, others want to take shorter day rides. Your success may depend on where you are and what your name recognition is. Being a musher who has the name Mackey can't hurt.

Keeping warm in my fur headgear.

Struggling to survive

We stalled in a blinding storm on the frozen sea ice. The dogs refused to move. I was shocked when I walked up to the front—open water!

Getting a hug at the finish line in Nome in 1977.

IN 1975, WE HAD NO IDEA what the race would become a quarter-century later. Back then, if you mentioned "the Iditarod" to anyone in the Lower 48 likely you would have gotten a puzzled look. The Iditarod wasn't on TV. You didn't see Iditarod documentaries. The early champions were unknown.

Now, I spend part of the winter in Arizona, which attracts people from all over the U.S. and Canada. Everywhere you go, people know about the Iditarod. Some people are surprisingly well informed. Rarely do you find someone who has never heard of it.

One winter I gave a lecture on the Iditarod. Five hundred people came. That shows how far the race has come, and how popular it is today.

In 1975, we were still educating the Alaska public. Heck, the participants were educating *themselves*. You never stop learning. You never stop advancing, which is what I was trying to do in 1976—advance in the standings.

After Emmitt Peters ran his swift race in 1975, the pace slowed again the next year because of the weather. That was the first year I thought I was capable of winning, though I finished eighth.

From the start, I was one of the frontrunners. Essentially, I led that race to Elim, more than nine hundred miles in. Penny, my leader for a fourth year, was the main reason I felt good about my chances, and basically I had the same team as the year before.

Training conditions were favorable—good trails, enough snow. Rick had run the race the year before, and the experience taught him something. He gave me encouragement like, "Man, you've got a good dog team, dad."

I figured I was smart enough to avoid mistakes made in previous years. I was the first team into every checkpoint for hundreds of miles. The dogs seemed to be getting better every day.

By the time I got to Unalakleet on the Bering Sea I had a seven and one-half hour lead. I was feeling good about myself and about the dogs. A storm was rolling in, but I thought I could make it to Shaktoolik. Then, if I could get out of Shaktoolik and reach Koyuk, I might have it made if the others were pinned down by the storm. It's only forty-two miles from Unalakleet to Shaktoolik, but it might as well have been a thousand.

Out of Unalakleet you go up over mountains. After about fifteen miles you drop down into an old reindeer station, where there is a corral, slaughterhouse, and a building that had housed the people who managed the herd. It is a big, wooden, two-story building, but abandoned. The weather got progressively worse. I was racing to stay ahead of the other dog teams and the storm, too. But I can tell you, the wind and snow were moving faster than any of us.

My movements were complicated by the location of the trail. That year it went out onto the frozen sea, a notoriously bad place. The trail fell apart more quickly on the open sea ice. The storm was powerful, but I had faith in my leader so I kept going into the night.

The wind got so strong it felt like a hurricane. All of a sudden, we stalled. The wind was howling in the dark. I let out a yell, but the dogs would not move. I walked to the front of the team to see if I could get them going. Visibility was about two inches. When I reached Penny, I was in for a shock. She had brought the dogs to a halt at the edge of open water! Smart dog. She saved us. But I didn't know what to do. There was no trail ahead, and I couldn't see a thing.

I grabbed Penny by the collar and said, "Let's go home." She turned the team around and led me back to the reindeer building. I opened the door and drove the dogs right inside. It was about eleven o'clock, and I wasn't going anywhere. I had my camp for the night.

I fed the dogs, cooked a bit, and curled up in the sleeping bag. I was waiting for daylight, not thinking too much, hoping I could find a trail and not venture off a cliff the next day. I wasn't worried about the competition. I figured the others wouldn't leave Unalakleet until the next morning because of the storm.

About seven-thirty the next morning, the storm was abating, and I prepared to leave. The dogs were all lined up in harness when they pricked up their ears. There came Victor Kotongan, who wasn't racing that year, but who used the reindeer station for a fish camp. He was leading four or five teams, guiding them because the trail had been wiped out. Jerry Riley's team was one of them. As soon as they came in, Victor turned around and mushed back the way he had come, but now I had plenty of company. Everyone was back in the race.

Victor helped them out as a favor because he knew the country. This was not against the rules. Officially it was OK, but I didn't like it one bit. There went my seven and one-half hour lead.

I was still the first one into Shaktoolik. And I was first into Koyuk and Elim, too. I thought I was going to win. My dogs were well-rested, and I should have fallen in behind the other teams instead of leading. Instead of being gung-ho I should have taken my time getting back the lead. But I was impatient. After four years, I still hadn't learned.

About ten miles out of Elim you climb sharply. The place is called Little McKinley. Halfway up into the hills, Riley passed me. This didn't bother me at the time, but later I learned Riley had left Elim *thirty minutes* behind me, and had made up that time on the trail. Being passed had a terrible psychological effect on my dogs. They decided the race was over. I was fourth into Golovin.

You could see the dogs were demoralized, moving slower and slower. So I just sat in Golovin. All kinds of mushers caught me there—Warner Vent, Harry Sutherland, Bud Smyth, and Emmitt Peters. Everybody was ready to rest except for Riley. He didn't stay long, and this paid off for him. He won.

Winning wasn't in the cards. Then some others passed me. Ralph Mann beat me by eight minutes. Sonny Nelson beat me by seven minutes. I was eighth, about three hours behind second. Still, the way things fell apart in Golovin I felt fortunate to be where I was.

But my appetite had been whetted. I saw how I could win the thing.

That year there was an interesting newcomer—a fellow named Rick Swenson, who finished tenth. Since then Rick won the Iditarod five times and, of course he was the guy I was running next to down Front Street in 1978. He was a rookie in 1976. He moved to Alaska from Minnesota and I remember meeting him when he was just a kid, working as a handler in 1968 when I went to St. Paul.

As a rookie, Rick was in awe of some of us. At that point Ken Chase and I were the only ones who had run all four Iditarods. He said, "You guys were my heroes." Well, he was a quick learner.

Rick had absolute dedication. He bought a bunch of dogs from good mushers, including Joe Redington Sr. He had the foresight to talk to people and to learn. Truly he was a student of dog mushing. It means a lot to me that I beat him in 1978 because he was the defending champion. And when my son Rick won in 1983, Swenson was the defending champion then, too. Nobody could have predicted that this guy would show up from Minnesota, and become Iditarod champion his second year.

This was about the time a newspaperman from London, Ian Woolrich, came to Alaska to cover the Iditarod. He called it "The Last Great Race on Earth." That name stuck. It makes no difference whether it's true. It's part of the mystique.

Maybe the Yukon Quest is run over tougher terrain, but the Iditarod captures the public's imagination. The Iditarod has the most competitive depth, it gets more media coverage, and the purse is bigger. But the purse wasn't always there.

In the early years, even though it was announced as the richest sled-dog race ever, the Iditarod was not a financial bonanza for the racers. Jerry Riley's first-place purse in 1976 was only $7,200, the lowest ever. In 1977, when Rick Swenson captured his first title, he won $9,600. It was a battle to get established.

What really helped us is when artist Jon Van Zyle painted a picture that became an official Iditarod poster. Jon competed in the race twice and was inspired by it. He wasn't nearly as famous then as he is now, but his Iditarod work became popular and raised a lot of money for the race. What he did was great. If you knew the trail, you could look at one of his paintings and know exactly where that scene was. His work stirred the imagination of the fans. I've got Jon Van Zyle Iditarod pictures hanging in my living room today. He still paints a picture for the annual Iditarod poster. His help has been tremendous.

Fred Machetanz, one of the greatest Alaska artists of all time, helped as well. Fred let us use his paintings on the covers of the early Iditarod annuals.

Later he donated a picture that became a signed and limited edition print with signatures of the early winners. That sold out and raised a lot of badly needed money. That led to Charles Gause becoming an official Iditarod artist, and his work raised more money for the Iditarod. But in the beginning, Jon Van Zyle's pictures helped broaden the acceptance and awareness of the Iditarod beyond Alaska.

Someone who played an important role in bringing the Iditarod to the world was Peter Henning, who came to Alaska as a producer for ABC-TV. When the network stopped televising the Iditarod, Peter became affiliated with other companies. Each year he helped produce documentaries. Some years you would watch it and think, "Gee, that's informative for someone who doesn't know anything about the Iditarod." Other times, when the finish wasn't even close, you might think, "Wow, he made that a race."

Finances were tight in 1976. Jerry Riley was the only winner who never got the full prize money he earned. He was supposed to get $12,000. It wasn't much better for Swenson in 1977. The Iditarod was established on the calendar in early March, but those of us on the board never knew if the race was going to survive.

There were all kinds of suggestions about what to do—run every other year, pay smaller purses. It was even suggested that we not run all the way to Nome so the expense wouldn't be as great.

We were able to get more in-kind donations. That helped. And people like Jon Van Zyle and Fred Machetanz made a difference. That's what kept the Iditarod going. Nobody involved with the race got paid for anything. I put hundreds of hours on my airplane and paid for the fuel. You paid your own phone bills.

In 1980, the year after I was president of the organization, the new president, Al Crane, asked me, "What do you figure it cost you to be president." More than $7,000, I told him, and he laughed. He didn't believe me. Before the end of his term, he told me, "I've surpassed $7,000. This is expensive!"

Seeing Alaska from the air

Joe Redington disappeared flying to Galena. His son wanted to call search and rescue, but Vi said no, Joe always said if anything happened to give him a week.

Out on the trail in 1985. I was race manager that year.

I BOUGHT an airplane in the mid-1970s, having taken up flying while doing construction contracting in the Bush. Often I flew guys who worked for me into the small communities where I had contracts.

However, my four-seat Cessna 180 became an Iditarod plane, too. One year, I helped fly the British Broadcasting Company crew along the trail. But I rarely flew just for the fun of it. I went from Point A to Point B with a purpose. The Cessna was the first of four airplanes I owned. I survived them all. In Alaska, that's saying something. In a place where the weather is so volatile, there are always close calls, or worse. Often weather is the cause. Or pilot error.

I helped search for Joe Redington—twice. Joe used to joke that he had crashed ten times, but always got back up in the air. He believed if he got himself into trouble, he could get himself out—and usually he did. Joe's most publicized crash had to do with the Iditarod. He was flying to a board meeting in Galena and never showed up.

We had planned to fly to Galena together, each of us in our own plane. After the meeting, I was going on to Nome for something. He was headed for Unalakleet. We were going to leave on a Friday, but he called me the night before and said, "I just got hung up and can't go tomorrow, so I'm going to leave Saturday morning." I went to the meeting on my own. Then, Joe's plans changed again and he got away on Friday afternoon, but I didn't know that.

The meeting took place in Galena without Joe, but we were not unduly worried. Joe always had a lot going on, and we figured he had been sidetracked. I was back home on Monday evening when the phone rang. It was Joee Redington. He asked, "How did the meeting go?" I said, "What do you mean? Haven't you talked to your dad?" Joe hadn't been heard from in three days.

I drove over to the Redingtons and told Joe's wife, Vi, that Joe hadn't arrived in Galena. Joee wanted to call search and rescue right away, but Vi said no, Joe always said if anything happened to give him a week. Some of us flew out anyway searching for Joe. We didn't see anything and when we came back, Vi called call search and rescue. Soon the whole state was looking for Joe.

True to his word, though, Joe got himself out of trouble. His engine had quit on him, and when he was bringing the plane in for a landing in the wilderness, he bent a propeller. He fixed the engine, straightened the prop, and got back in the air. Then he made another forced landing. In all, the engine quit three times, he repaired it each time, and flew into Nenana.

Vi drove the couple of hundred miles up the Parks Highway to pick him up. First thing Joe said to her was, "What the hell did you call search and rescue for?"

Wilford Ryan Jr. of Ryan Air administered my long-distance solo for flight certification in 1976. At the time I was building a hangar for his dad. I flew from Unalakleet to Kaltag, down the Yukon River to Grayling, where Ernie Chase signed my logbook, then back over the mountains to Unalakleet.

I flew for about fifteen years, logging more than two thousand hours as a licensed pilot after putting in more than one thousand hours of unlicensed flying time. I sold my last plane in 1990. I walked away from it. If you fly long enough you're going to do something stupid or you're going to get ambushed by the weather. Things happen fast.

Around 1979, I had a close call. I took a load of horse feed up to the Rainy Pass Lodge and picked up a horse wrangler for the flight back. I was headed for Wasilla when we ran into a snow squall. We landed to wait it out at an airstrip twenty miles northwest of Skwentna. Then we took off again and another squall came up near Big Lake. Soon the sky was like the inside of a milk bottle. I couldn't see a thing.

Think of getting ice all over the windshield of your car and trying to see out through spaces in the steering wheel. That's what it was like. I was descending lower and lower trying to look underneath the clouds and snow and suddenly I was flying right into it. I made a 180-degree turn and soon I was experiencing vertigo and had lost my sense of direction. The next thing I saw was a yard light next to someone's house right in front of me.

I was closing the gap quickly between plane and house. It was tense. I punched the power and pulled back on the yoke. It's a wonder I didn't stall. I was paying attention to the instruments when I spotted a road. I hollered at my passenger, "Don't lose track of that road!" Then I started curving around flying in and out of snow squalls and landed on the Parks Highway. Just banged her right down on the road. Mile fifty-eight. I was about six miles south of Earl Norris's place.

I pulled into someone's driveway to get off the road. The wrangler got out and knelt down on the ground shaking like a leaf. The people in the house came running out to see what the commotion was all about, and I borrowed a phone to call home. Iditarod photographer Bill Devine drove over with my wife to pick me up.

The weather was clear when I went back to pick up the airplane. God, I had landed a few yards from power lines. I had been lucky. A few days later I talked with a friend, Cliff Hudson, the Bush pilot from Talkeetna. "Cliff," I said, "I did everything wrong." And he said, "Nah, you did one thing right." I said, "What's that?" He said, "You survived."

One of the other planes I owned had belonged to Don Sheldon, who, like Cliff, became well known flying mountain climbers in and out of the Mount McKinley area and taking part in some impressive rescues. Don took a wing off this plane on the side of McKinley. It was salvaged, brought down from the mountain, and rebuilt with a new engine. A pilot named Larry Mitchell owned it for a while and outfitted it with floats. Nice airplane.

I used to fly from Wasilla to Nome all of the time. Sometimes I followed the Yukon River and Bering Sea Coast. I got a whole new perspective on that country that I had driven through with dog teams. I learned to have greater respect for the weather as a pilot. There were fewer places to wait out the weather. And if you pushed it, the weather would get you.

Another time the wind was blowing when I took off from Unalakleet. I was putting up a building in St. Michael for Jerry Austin, another Iditarod musher. Well, the wind worsened. I radioed to Jerry about the severe headwinds, and he said it was blowing about seventy mph at St. Michael. I asked him to round up a dozen people to grab the plane and hold it down when I landed.

It was thrilling to fly over the Iditarod Trail and see it in a different perspective. In some ways studying the overall terrain from the air was helpful to me when I ran the Iditarod. I could see that I should be on this side of a hill or that side of a ravine or valley. Flying made me more aware of where I was on the ground, and how long it would take to get somewhere.

My most fascinating connection between land and sky occurred when Joe Redington and I received a state Department of Natural Resources contract in 1980 to mark brush on the Iditarod Trail for surveyors. Joe was on a dog sled and I did most of the flying. You could see the trail from the air even when you had no idea where it was on the ground.

I talked to him on a radio and said, "Joe, you're standing right in the middle of the old trail." He said, "I can't see anything." He asked which way he should move and I told him.

We discovered that the people who put in the original trail never went out into the open unless they had to. If they could stay in the woods, they did. Everything was in straight lines. They never wound around a hill. They went right over it. They avoided open ground where wind and snow would erase a trail. Most of the people who went over the old Iditarod Trail walked it.

When you're traveling the trail between Anchorage and Nome on the back of a dog sled the country is so vast, you feel insignificant. If the weather is good, with bright sunshine, or clear moonlight, it's beautiful. And if your dogs are feeling good and running well, there is nothing more beautiful.

You see things from the back of a dog sled. You're off the highway system. You're closer to the land. When you're flying, you get a greater perspective of the awesome feat it is to cover it by dog sled. You're reminded how big Alaska is.

I remember flying once to Unalakleet where Joe Redington worked at the fish plant and ending up at Nome. I had gotten into some bad weather when I started out and once you leave McGrath you're screwed if you're headed cross-country because there's nowhere to set down. Out in the middle of nowhere, I got bullheaded. Instead of swinging east and heading to another village I decided I was going to push on and, boy, it got hairy—dense clouds, lousy visibility.

This was one of my many airplanes.

I finally found the Yukon River, flew upriver, and landed at Kaltag. Then I decided to take a short cut through a pass and head for Golovin, but I missed it. Later I learned the villagers had heard my engine and wondered why I didn't land. But I never saw the village. When I got to the coast, I turned north, still thinking I would find Golovin. No way. I was barely able to follow the shoreline, flying twenty feet off the water. And I was getting low on fuel.

I finally situated myself, but I wasn't in any position to land in Golovin, so I kept going to Cape Nome. I called the flight service and the guy said, "We're shut down." I said, "Really?"

The guy seemed to realize I was in trouble and asked what were my intentions. I asked for special permission to come in despite lack of minimum required visibility. I didn't know if I had enough fuel. Both my gauges were flat empty.

Suddenly I flew past the KNOM radio tower, and we were talking back and forth about how little visibility I had. I admitted it was pretty bad. I was upset. The situation was tight. Should I fly over the city and run out of fuel, or land on the road? He said, "Let me know when you see the runway lights." Pretty quickly, I said, "I see them." He came back on the radio and said, "Where are you?" And I said, "I just landed."

I went into town for the night. The next morning I checked the fuel. I had one rung on a three-pound coffee can left. Whew.

On the trail with Joe

We had to cross open water. I hollered, and the dogs plunged in. Immediately they were swept downstream, and I was standing in icy water up to my waist.

I'll never forget borrowing a lamp from Joe Redington.

SPENDING TIME on the trail with Joe Redington was always special. Sometimes he helped me. Sometimes I helped him. Or we just had adventures together.

During the 1974 race, Joe saved my bacon. Five miles out of Knik, on an icy place on the trail, I snapped a runner and stanchions off one side of the sled. I turned the team around, which wasn't hard, but then I was heading back to the Knik checkpoint with twenty-three teams coming the opposite way. That *was* hard.

The dogs never faltered. They thought we were going home. It was amazing the job they did passing all those teams with a heavy sled. The other drivers didn't appreciate me. It was as if I was driving the wrong way on a one-way street.

We made it to Knik without incident. Joe had just arrived at the checkpoint, which is just down the street from his homestead. He had taken a big sled out of Anchorage for the 50-mile ride to Knik and then switched it for another sled. He gave me the first sled, and that's the one I took all the way to Nome.

I took off from Knik Lake again and passed almost all of the teams again by the time we got to Susitna Station. I had a good team—and a good friend in Joe.

In 1976, Joe and I were traveling together when he got into trouble. We left the Rainy Pass Lodge and reached the traditional camping spot at Hell's Gate. It was about five o'clock, and I was prepared to stop for the night. Joe said he wanted to continue on to Rohn. So I figured if he was going to keep going, I would too.

We had flown over the Rohn River several times leading up to the race, and we knew there were problems with overflow. It was going to be a tough go. We'd no sooner started than his headlamp broke. We'd been under way maybe thirty minutes. Mushers these days carry spare batteries and headlamps, but in the first years of the race most of us stopped for the night when darkness fell. You didn't run at night. A headlamp was insurance in case you were caught out in the dark before reaching your camp.

I was leading the way, and Joe was guiding his team by the light of my headlamp. Pretty soon my battery died. Well, Joe had a bad headlamp and a good battery, so he gave me the battery. We were within a mile of Rohn. The trail followed down the right bank of the river and then made a portage off the ice about three hundred feet up and over the bank.

Joe fell behind. Without the headlamp he had trouble navigating. I had Penny in lead, and she went where the trail should have gone and stopped. I parked the sled, went up front to investigate, and realized the trail did not go over the bank. I left the dogs and walked back to see where we had lost the trail. Joe Delia and Frank Harvey were the trailbreakers, and I found where they had taken the snowmachines across the river. The problem was twenty feet of open water about a foot deep.

The only way across was through the river. So I turned the dogs around even though they did not want to go into the water. But they did respond, and we got through the open water onto solid ice beyond. Unfortunately, we ran into another twenty feet of open water. It was deeper and flowing fast. This was the main channel of the river. But I had no choice. I hollered to the team to go, and it plunged in. Immediately the dogs were swept downstream, and I was standing in water up to my waist.

I wrestled the team and the sled up onto the shelf ice on the opposite bank, but the dogs were going wild. I had my hands full and I was soaked. The dogs took off and got hung up in willow brush, creating a horrible tangle. It was chaotic for a few minutes. Then we rejoined the trail, which had wound back onto the river ice. I figured the Rohn checkpoint was about ten minutes away.

Then, I looked at the team, and my heart just about stopped. I was dragging a dog in harness. I stopped the team and ran to this dog, which showed no signs of life. Oh, God. I scooped up the dog. It was encrusted in ice from running through the water. So was I. I placed the dog in the sled and mushed into Rohn.

Lloyd Hessler and Sly Rabinski were the checkers. Delia and Harvey, the trailbreakers, were there. So was Dick Tozier. I told them what had happened at the river and officially reported having a dead dog. A ham radio operator was there and he spread the bad news. After the commotion died down, I remembered that Joe was right behind me. The whole fracas back on the trail had taken about fifteen minutes as I worked my way through a couple of hundred feet of trail. I hadn't seen Joe since then, but assumed he was coming.

I tended the dogs, got them warmed up, fed, and bedded down, and then I ducked into a warm cabin and collapsed. Later, somebody woke me up and said, "Hey, Joe's not here yet. Are you sure he was right behind you?" That's when I realized something was wrong. I jumped up, went outside, and there sat my dead dog—alive! I had put the dog next to the cabin when I went in. It was sitting up. I guess it had just passed out. What a comeback. This was the only dog that came back to life after being reported as dead. That dog ran all the way to Nome, and later I sold it to Brian Blanford, who ran the dog in his rookie Iditarod the following year.

By then three or four hours had passed, and Joe still wasn't in. That worried me. The snowmachiners couldn't go anywhere. Their machines were cakes of ice, and wouldn't start. I hooked up five dogs and steered them back onto the river. As soon as we got going, I saw Joe headed my way. Boy, did he have a tale of woe. He told me that when I left the shelf ice on the riverbank, his dogs kept going straight ahead into the water. Joe fell into a deep hole over his head. It was a wonder he not only lived to tell the story but also didn't lose a dog.

He used the ice to help pull himself out. But he was still in trouble. He was soaking wet and shivering. You can get hypothermia in minutes. He managed to get a fire going. Later, he told me that it was the closest call he'd ever had.

Joe was angry that I hadn't gone back to look for him sooner. But we were good enough friends that when I told him my story, he understood the situation. Even after Rohn we ran together as far as Koyuk. Then he dropped behind and finally scratched. I didn't know he quit the race. Joe flew off the trail to Nome. When I saw him at the finish line, I said, "Ain't that something? Joe beat me to Nome."

Joe and I were together on the Iditarod Trail often during races. In 1977, Joe was fifth and I was sixth.

After the 1976 race I had decided I was not going to be the rabbit. I led for a long time, but I didn't win. Things went wrong. Still, you reach a point where you learn that if you want to win, you have to know what's going on up ahead of you and you have to try to be there in the front group. After that, it's just how it unfolds. It's not hard to make a simple mistake that can cost you a race. You stop for an hour, maybe just to put new booties on your dogs' feet. That hour magnifies itself and you lose several places. And you find yourself unable to make up for the lost time.

You may not recognize these effects at the time. But you know if two people are running at the same speed and suddenly one loses thirty minutes, something happened. One musher might have a dog with a problem. He might have to load it into the sled and carry it for five miles. But you've got to do what you've got to do.

Sometimes strategy plays into it. One team might be an hour ahead of me. I might cut my dogs' rest by thirty minutes to catch up. I made up a half hour, but it could hurt me later. This kind of cat-and-mouse goes on all the time. That little bit of lost rest might translate into a bigger gap because of lack of freshness. The gap starts to expand and there's nothing you can do about it.

Take NASCAR racing. The announcer will say they've got five laps to go and three guys are bumper to bumper. Their order never changes in five laps. They just can't make up that one second on the driver in front, unless something goes wrong. It's the same way with dogs.

After a year when the times all slowed down, the 1977 race picked up speed again. The winning time was sixteen days plus. After four or five years, Iditarod mushers were learning how to race a long distance. The cooperation and understanding between drivers and veterinarians took a great leap. It used to be that mushers were tempted to avoid the vets. They were afraid they would have to drop dogs they needed if they had a little problem. Now the communication is much better and at the first sign of a problem the musher goes right to the vet for help.

In 1977, I thought I had a team capable of winning. I had new leaders—Teller, Shrew, and Skipper. Skipper turned out to be a ball of fire. He wanted to be in front.

I had a faster front end now with Penny retired, but it wasn't as reliable. Penny was a leader who, if she didn't see the trail, could *feel* the trail and never take a step off of it. With this new crew I had to have my wits about me. These leaders didn't have experience yet. It was a good race for us, though. You don't have to win to have a good race.

Rick Swenson, Jerry Riley, Warner Vent, and Emmitt Peters got a little ahead of us, but Joe and I stayed together for a lot of reasons. We usually agreed that we would run together, but whatever happened wouldn't hold us back and prevent us from going on and trying to beat one another. We were just good buddies who enjoyed each other's company. We had the same outlook on life in a lot of ways.

Joe developed a style of racing in which he would go like hell between checkpoints. Rarely would he stop. That wasn't always my way. I would take a break.

Yet, Joe wasn't as fast tending to business at the checkpoints. Joe got caught up talking to people He carried enough supplies for three mushers in his sled. Before a race I would say, "Joe, you've got to cut down on your load." He said, "Come on over to the house and tell me what I don't need." I said, "You don't need this and you don't need that." He agreed, and we set it all aside. Next thing you knew, he would take half of it and pack it back into the sled.

Joe Redington said he wanted to be prepared for anything, but he still didn't need so much stuff. We used to laugh about it, and Vi Redington would say, "Listen to what Dick's telling you." He'd just get that sheepish grin he had

Even with all of his gear, Joe could be like a wild man if he was in a hurry. Stand back! You'd get hurt with him throwing things around. He was so much fun to be with.

The checkpoints slowed him down too much. Joe was a man who didn't need much sleep. He hardly ever lay down in a bed. Instead he would make himself comfortable in a chair and doze off. After three or four hours, he was good for another day. He made up time by not sleeping as much as the other mushers.

Joe Redington was the darnedest guy I'd ever seen.

Now or never in 1978

*I resented it being said in some quarters that my
photo finish would be argued about for a long time.
Whatever little controversy there was blew over quickly.*

The 1978 finish may have been the most important second of my life.
©Rob Stapleton/Alaska Stock Images

WHEN TRAINING for the 1978 Iditarod began the previous fall, I told my wife I wanted to win. I would go anywhere to find snow for training. Little did I know where all this would lead.

I was living in Wasilla, which hadn't seen much snow. We had rain. So I piled the dogs into the truck and went to Eureka, or to Trapper Creek, or wherever. I drove hundreds of miles. I was active with the Iditarod committee, but I told Joe Redington my participation would be by long-distance telephone because I was training.

My team was coming into its prime. I had good dogs. I was forty-five, had confidence, and was fit mentally and physically. If I was going to do it, this was the year.

One of the places I trained was Point McKenzie. Quite a cast of characters camped on Joe's land. Joe trained there, too. So did Susan Butcher, who worked for Joe at his kennel. Others training were Shelly Vandiver, who later wrote children's books as Shelly Gill, and Varona Thompson. We had a good training environment, away from the hustle and bustle.

Varona had no intention of running a team after her 1977 rookie race, but agreed to help me with my team. She sold all of her dogs except for an old leader. Meanwhile, I broke my right shoulder in November. The dogs didn't run for two weeks. I hired a gal to go out there and train them with Varona. I was back home in Wasilla recuperating. I tried to fly back and forth every day to see how things were going.

Things weren't going well. After a run, one of the dogs killed another. So I got back out there. We trained two teams—my race team and the young dogs Varona would run. She followed me on a 50-mile trail. We never stopped. I remember her in tears one time insisting she had to stop and rest the dogs. I said, "Don't you dare stop." I wanted the dogs to set their own pace so they would go faster. This was my new strategy. By the time we finished the 50-mile runs, we'd cut our travel time in half.

Varona ran my team of thirteen young dogs in the Iditarod behind her old leader. At Susitna Station, her leader died—just keeled over—and she went the rest of the way with my young dogs. She ran with Susan Butcher, who placed nineteenth and became the first woman to finish in the money. Varona was twentieth.

This was Susan's rookie year. She was serious. She was a good learner, and Joe was a good teacher. Comparing Susan and Shelly, both living in the same tent and doing the same thing, you saw that Susan was head and shoulders above Shelly. Shelly was in over her head. You didn't know where Susan was going to finish, but you were confident she would.

You thought, "Oh boy, if Shelly makes it, it'll be a miracle." But Shelly pulled it off. She placed twenty-ninth. Not that I saw Shelly race. I was the old-timer up front.

Nowadays the top contenders are in their forties. In most other sports, that's old, but not in long-distance mushing

Rick Swenson was eighteen years younger than me. In most sports, that's tough to compete with. I wasn't as large as Swenson either. If the contest were to lift a block of cement, he'd beat me. But we were racing sled dogs and had evenly matched teams. I beat him by out-snookering him. Having more experience was the only advantage I had.

It's no secret that back then Rick had a good-sized ego. He was defending champion. I'm this old guy whom he had looked up to and respected, but now he was going to whip me.

I'm the first one to admit he had a more controllable dog team than I did. I had a stronger team. As long as he led the most difficult part of the trail, I could out-run him. I realized that early on, before we got to McGrath. I used the whole race. That's the only way I beat him. But no one would ever do that to him again.

I had an awesome team. When I walked out the door of the checkpoint, every dog would jump to its feet, ready to go. I didn't even have to say anything.

I had finished sixth the year before. I didn't think there was much difference between sixth and first. To finish that high in the standings, everything's got to go just right. That's been the story of the race. Whoever makes the fewest mistakes is going to be a contender, and a little luck helps too.

I resented it being said in some quarters that my photo finish ahead of Swenson that year would be argued about for a long time. Whatever little controversy there was blew over quickly.

The next year I chaired the Iditarod Rules Committee, and Rick Swenson insisted that we put in a rule of what constituted a finish. It had not been addressed specifically before.

Our finishing time was fast. We came across in fourteen days and eighteen hours. That put us back to the speed Emmitt generated in 1975. The funny thing is it was generally agreed the Iditarod would not be run any faster. Now people are sure that one of these years somebody's going to get to Nome in less than nine days.

The speed of the race was not the focus, though. The one-second finish was on everybody's mind. There had never been anything like it and there hasn't been again. It made a huge impact. One of the first calls I got was from Sydney, Australia. The headline in every paper focused on the photo finish. The race was a thousand miles, and people couldn't imagine how it would turn out to be so close.

There was a German film crew at the finish that almost cost me the race. I got tangled with their tripod. Afterwards, the director told me, "You just won me a gold medal." Joe Redington, who was behind us and finished fifth, said, "If I had known what was going to happen, I'd have scratched just to have been there."

Joe said it was the greatest moment in the history of the race.

Once was enough 18

When I was Iditarod Trail Committee president, we discussed the future of the race. Where did we want to go with it? How could we improve it?

Son Rick and two of his favorite dogs.

A YEAR LATER I didn't even defend my title.

People asked me how could I skip the Iditarod a year after winning. I had several reasons. I became president of the Iditarod Trail Committee and had no time to train. And, having won, I had no hunger to win again.

I had been working for the committee for years. When I took over as president I wanted to do a good job. The Iditarod was changing. We were more established. We got more attention. The media was solidly behind us. Financially we had gotten onto more solid ground. We had many discussions about marketing and about the future. Where did we want to go? What could we do to improve the race? How could we raise money?

We knew we had weak spots. We needed better dog care. We wanted to have more veterinarians on the trail. We wanted to work more closely with our volunteer pilots, called the Iditarod Air Force, flying out dropped dogs.

We had been working out of Dorothy Page's house. Now we had an office over Teeland's store in Wasilla. We hired an office employee—Cathy Thompson, who later would become my wife. There was a lot to do.

I admit that as a competitor I had lost my edge. It was my goal to win the Iditarod and I did. I didn't need to win it again, but I wanted to be part of the race. In 1979, I stayed close. I served as a race judge and was one of three pilots and a technical advisor for a BBC film crew.

I flew the co-producers, Tony Salmon and Susan Ruddy, all over. It was fun to show features of the Iditarod Trail to people who were seeing it for the first time. It felt good, like a homecoming, when we landed at Joe Delia's in Skwentna. This was my first experience with broadcasting other than being interviewed.

After the race, I spent four weeks in London helping edit the film. During that time I had four days free and spent it in Wales, ending up on a sheep ranch riding a horse. Then I rented a Cessna 172 and flew to an island off the coast of southern England. No sooner had I taken off than I lost electrical power. The radio didn't work. The flaps didn't work. Nothing. Below, everything looked the same. You looked down and there were rolling hills and a little church steeple and a bunch of buildings. Then you looked over to the next little valley and it was the same thing. I had no idea where I was.

Then I noticed a huge grass landing strip. So I dumped the plane right down onto that strip. I needed to know where I was and what was wrong with the plane. As soon as I landed, four vehicles came racing up to me with sirens and lights. I had landed at a camouflaged, somewhat secret military base. The landing strip was more sophisticated than it appeared from the air.

I was taken to the local provost who demanded to know what on earth I was doing. Their expressions said, "Uh, huh, another Yank," but they weren't laughing. They had no sense of humor about this at all. They told me I had violated all kinds of laws. They questioned the flying club about the Cessna rental and contacted Tony Salmon at the BBC to verify my story about why I was in England. I was in custody for a couple of hours.

When I didn't enter the Iditarod in 1979, my son Rick took six of my dogs and blended them into his team. He finished eighth. That was a good performance, but at the time he didn't think so. He put himself under terrible pressure because he was running a lot of the same dogs I had run the year before.

By the time Rick reached McGrath, his dogs were horribly ill. They picked up a virus and they wouldn't eat or drink. But they were hydrated and rejuvenated in McGrath. He had a team again. He did well.

When the 1980 race rolled around I was ready to get back into it, just for the fun of it. I still had no hunger to win. What I remember most clearly about the race that year was an unscheduled stop in Koyukuk, which was not an official checkpoint. The people insisted that several of us come into the village for a meal. So we did, not wanting to offend them. We all got food poisoning. Afterward, we were going down the trail and vomiting and feeling awful. What a terrible time! I scratched at Unalakleet. Joe Redington and Sonny Lindner, who had eaten in Koyukuk, too, also scratched that year.

I shipped the dogs back to Wasilla and had my airplane brought out to me. That's when a plane crash killed a Spanish film crew following the race. Sonny Lindner and I saw it go down. We landed on the ice and walked to the scene. That was tough. I went into Nome and became ill all over again.

My illness turned out to be more than food poisoning. I had ruptured my stomach. As you're running along the trail, especially in rough spots, you're always getting banged around. I never knew what happened.

The doctors thought I had damaged my stomach eleven days earlier and had been bleeding internally ever since. I needed blood transfusions and was in tough shape. I was in the hospital for about nine days, but I always regretted scratching. That's the only time I didn't finish an Iditarod.

I caused the Iditarod considerable heartache once with something I said. It wasn't a misquote, but the quote was incomplete. I was asked what mindset it takes to win the Iditarod. I said it takes one hundred percent dedication. Absolutely nothing can stand in your way. You must have an attitude, "I am going to win this Iditarod come hell or high water. Nothing is going to deter me. If the dogs and I cross the finish line and drop dead, it's OK as long as I've won the race." But I went on to say that wasn't going to happen, though you had to have that kind of *attitude*. Oh, the reaction was tremendous from animal-rights groups. Dick Mackey said this and Dick Mackey said that. You can't ever change it. Once a quote is out there like that, you're on the defensive.

I never recaptured the hunger to win again. To me, the remarkable thing about those who kept winning—Rick Swenson, Susan Butcher, Martin Buser, Jeff King and Doug Swingley—is how they stayed focused and hungry.

What an accomplishment to win again and again. I salute them all.

A new challenge at Coldfoot

Coldfoot became a truckers' place. Hundreds of trucks drove the highway, and nearly every one stopped. If a trucker drove past, he got onto the CB radio and apologized!

The modest start of Coldfoot Services in June 1981.

LITTLE DID I SUSPECT in 1981 that my life was about to change dramatically. I was wed to the Iditarod. I was a construction man by trade. Who would have guessed I was going to become known for operating a gas station?

Construction was not going well. I had my own company, but I was getting shut out on key bids. I was race manager of the Iditarod that year, and the race was over. My marriage wasn't doing well.

One day I saw an intriguing newspaper ad inviting proposals for a state contract up north. The state was looking for someone to fabricate thirty-four bear-proof garbage cans, place the cans along the Dalton Highway, and then collect the garbage over the summer.

The Dalton Highway, known as the Haul Road because supplies were trucked on it to Prudhoe Bay, was an isolated strip running from a remote junction south of the Yukon River north through the Brooks Range to the Arctic Ocean.

The state legislature had opened the highway to the public. According to the state constitution, any road maintained with public funds has to be open to the public. Gov. Jay Hammond responded by opening it during June, July, and August as far as Dietrich Camp on the south side of Atigun Pass.

The oil companies built the road and then turned it over to the state after the trans-Alaska Pipeline was built. The state got five hundred miles of free road, but had to take responsibility for its maintenance in a rough, remote country far from the existing highway system.

The contract was one of several being let for the three-month opening. One contract was for construction of pullouts. Another was building fiberglass toilets. At that time there was a state camp at the Yukon Crossing. Whoever won the contract would haul garbage on a regular schedule from Dietrich Camp to Yukon, a round-trip of three hundred miles. I decided I would go after the contract.

The Dalton Highway starts at Livengood, seventy-five miles north of Fairbanks. This is where the Elliott Highway turns west toward Minto and Manley. This is pretty country, but pretty empty, too. The Yukon Crossing is at Mile 56. Coldfoot is at Mile 175. Dietrich Camp was about two hundred miles north of Livengood.

The brother-in-law of a friend had recently arrived from California and needed a start. I told him if I got the contract, I would put new tires on his pickup, provide gas and oil, and pay him $10,000 for the summer. He'd been making five dollars an hour at a factory, so this sounded like a Godsend to him. I was still running a construction business, so he drove to Fairbanks from Wasilla to submit my bid.

In the middle of the afternoon he called to say the contract was mine. I won by twenty-two dollars on a bid of a little over $30,000.

Next thing you know, with the help of friend Charlie Graham, we were manufacturing garbage cans from fifty-five gallon drums. We attached handles to the top, like those on mailboxes, to keep out the bears. The cans had to be in place by June 1 for the opening of the highway. On the last day of May, I joined with the highway superintendent driving up the road distributing garbage cans.

It was ten o'clock at night by the time we reached Dietrich Camp. The camp was for state employees only, closed to everyone else. I said, "Dang, you can't even get a cup of coffee on this highway." He said, "Well, they did let out a permit back down at Coldfoot, but the guy wasn't interested in running a cafe. He was more interested in fuel sales, but it's not going to materialize." The operation was supposed to start the next day, and the guy with the permit hadn't shown up.

Don Burt, a long-time Iditarod volunteer, heard I was driving up the Dalton Highway and had come along for company. When we passed Coldfoot headed south, I was thinking, "Wouldn't it be nice to have that permit for the summer?"

Don owned a blue paddy wagon bus that he hauled around to the Alaska State Fair in Palmer and the Tanana Valley Fair in Fairbanks. I suggested to Don, "You could bring the paddy wagon up here, sell hamburgers, and kick back for the summer." Don said he didn't have money to get started. I had some money saved up for the construction season, but I was sick of construction. I figured I'd take three months off and then get back into dogs in the fall.

At that time there was almost nothing left of Coldfoot, just trees. The highway was rough, with horrendous rocks sticking up in the roadway. You couldn't call it a gravel road because it wasn't that smooth. On this rock highway we passed the remnants of an old town fifty-nine miles north of the Arctic Circle. That was the first time I saw Coldfoot. All that was left from the past were a few buildings in serious disrepair and an old cemetery. An abandoned construction camp remained intact from pipeline construction days of the 1970s.

At the turn of the Twentieth Century, Coldfoot was a bustling community. Gold was discovered there in 1899. I've seen pictures of Coldfoot with forty-seven buildings visible, and that wasn't even the whole community. Northern Commercial Co. had a store there and there were several other stores, brothels, and numerous saloons. It was a boomtown. But it didn't last. It petered out about 1922. Everything moved up the road about a dozen miles to Wiseman. Wiseman survived. Coldfoot did not.

I drove to the Bureau of Land Management in Fairbanks and learned that the Coldfoot permit-holder was not going to fulfill terms of the permit. I said I wanted the permit, but was told three or four people were ahead of me. I said, "Well, they're not here and I am."

After a conversation they asked me how soon I could be in Coldfoot. I said, "What do I have to do?"

They wanted me to sell regular and unleaded gasoline and make tire repairs for the traveling public. We made a deal: If I could be there by June 15, the permit was mine. All they promised was three months.

Timing is everything. Up to five hundred trucks were running the road every day. The drivers were carrying brown bag lunches. With that knowledge, I knew I could make a go of it.

I bought an ancient Ford fuel truck and headed north hauling gasoline. Don came along in his pale blue paddy wagon. His partner was driving a green Dodge truck, pulling a camper trailer. What a convoy! We had tents too and stuff you wouldn't believe.

As we drove north, passing truckers hailed us on the CB radio asking what we were doing. I told them we were headed for Coldfoot to set up a cafe, and added, "What are you going to have?" They wanted hamburgers, hot dogs, and soup. This was my first advertising blitz.

It was seven-thirty at night on June 15 when we arrived at the Coldfoot gravel pit. There was a little slough nearby. That's where we got our water. We were dead tired. We had driven all the way from Wasilla, more than 550 miles, in junk transport. The next morning when we woke up, more than one hundred truckers and their rigs were parked at the gravel pit wanting to know when they could get something to eat.

We hadn't even hooked up the propane tanks. I said, "Ding, ding, ding," and we were off and running. Once we started feeding people the biggest problem was hauling enough supplies from Fairbanks to keep going. Although we were having marital problems, Kathie helped by hauling supplies from Anchorage. Camping at Coldfoot, even for only three months, was the last straw, however. She wasn't alone thinking this was crazy. My banker was aghast that I would give up construction for this hare-brained enterprise.

Soon, I was back at the BLM office. Could I operate Coldfoot the coming winter? The answer was no. "Why not?" I asked. A newly minted employee who didn't look old enough to shave told me, "That's cold country up there. You'd never survive." I got a little testy and said, "Let me tell you something, kid. I've slept on a trail in a dog sled more nights than you've slept in a bed. Don't tell me about cold." The response was, "It's your funeral. If you want to stay, go ahead."

The original permit was scheduled to expire September 1. We were operating out of an old school bus and I was living in a tent. Don and his partner were living in the old trailer. It was very crude, but it was a challenge, and I liked it.

We could expect sub-freezing weather by the middle of the month and permanent snow about two weeks later. We knew we had to prepare. The truckers helped us. Over time, many truckloads of drilling mud had been hauled north to Prudhoe Bay, most of it carried in three-quarter-inch plywood boxes. We used the plywood that truckers back-hauled from Prudhoe Bay and built a 16-by-24-foot box on the back end of the bus.

At first we served customers on seats inside the old bus. Others were outside on tree stumps balancing paper plates on their knees. Now we had a plywood cafe with a wood-burning barrel stove and a tarpaper shack for the few workers. I acquired a fifteen-foot camper trailer, too.

Although some people thought I was crazy, I was convinced Coldfoot would be a gold mine. We knew it soon was going to be sixty-something-below-zero, but we were still bringing in money.

In August, the Iditarod held a board meeting in Fairbanks. I was driving to it when a tire went flat in Livengood. By the time I arrived I had missed dinner. Cathy Thompson, who worked for the Iditarod, asked how I was doing and gave me a hug and a kiss. After the meeting, I hung around to eat, and Cathy and I had a drink. She asked what Coldfoot was like. I said it was hectic, but one of these days I would find a woman to go up there and live with me and work the place.

She blurted out, "I will." I looked at her kind of funny and said, "Really?"

I told her she didn't know what she was letting herself in for. She ought to come up and see for herself. She said, "OK." At that point we were just good friends. We had never been romantically inclined.

Cathy came for a visit and stayed. In January 1982 we got married—she became my third wife. Susan Butcher was Cathy's maid of honor. Joe Redington Sr. was my best man. In addition to a new wife, I gained three children, all girls. The eldest, Kaye, was attending college. Kim was fifteen and Kris seven. Later, Kim got married in Coldfoot, before moving to California.

It became apparent that Don and his partner and Cathy and I weren't going to work out together, so I bought out Don's interest. It was unclear what I was buying as I still had a temporary permit. But I believed the BLM would allow us to stay there long-term.

Although the original idea was to open the road for the public, we didn't see a dozen tourists all summer. Coldfoot became a truckers' place. It seemed as if just about every trucker stopped. If somebody drove past they got onto the CB radio and apologized! It was a place to talk with other truckers. The facilities were crude, but the stop gave them a chance to get out of the truck and relax a bit after driving hundreds of miles. The truckers could come into a place that was heated and have something to eat. It was nothing fancy, but it was a hot meal—hamburgers, hot dogs, chili, bacon and eggs, hot cakes, soups, and lots of coffee.

Oh, and there was an outhouse—the only one for five hundred miles!

Cold winters at Coldfoot

Thirty-five below is no problem. You bundle up. Forty-five below, hey, it's getting nippy. The real cold starts at fifty below. That's when you become real cautious.

Cathy and I worked almost around the clock at Coldfoot.

THE FIRST WINTER in Coldfoot I thought we were going to freeze to death. I've lived in cold places, but this was something else. By December it hit 60 degrees below zero. Regularly it was 35, 40, 45 below. And much of the time we had to work *outdoors*.

The state highway maintenance camp put in a well, and we hauled water from a mile away in fifty-five gallon drums. It didn't take long for ice to form inside the drums.

To the average person in the Lower 48, a temperature of 35 below is unbelievably cold. But if you are used to cold, 35 below is no problem.

You bundle up, wear gloves, and if you're moving around, you're basically OK. At 45 below, hey, it's getting nippy. At minus 50, man it's *cold*. That's when you become real cautious.

At 60 below, vehicles that sit for a while start to fail. You could plug in your truck for a while and the engine would start instantly, but if you didn't let the clutch out slowly you could pop the universal joint. And for the first few miles going down the road you would hear a thump, thump, thump. The tires felt like they were square. Of course, you left the trucks plugged in all the time. We had a bunch of junk trunks, but they started.

When you got inside the heat felt good. You have to move more slowly outdoors, and if you bang a finger at 50 below the hide comes off in a hurry. You cut and bruise yourself more easily. And you've got to cover your skin. It's easy to frostbite your face.

Severe cold is not hospitable. All work is done in slow motion. As I look back on it, Arizona wouldn't look as good as it does to me now if Coldfoot hadn't had such a harsh winter environment, and if we hadn't had to do so much outside.

Because Coldfoot is so far north, winter daylight is scarce. If it's not dark, it's dusk. You operate from ten to two quite nicely, but you need artificial light for the other twenty hours a day. The extreme cold works against you psychologically, too. You get set up and ready to work at ten o'clock. Then it's so cold you feel like you deserve a coffee break after an hour. Then it's time for lunch and, by the time you go back out in the afternoon, only thirty minutes of daylight remain.

I wasn't as affected by the cold as much as some of the employees. I had an interest in the place. Then I developed an even a bigger interest in Coldfoot in the spring of 1982 when the federal government granted me a thirty-year permit.

Coldfoot became my consuming interest, superseding my devotion to the Iditarod. I was committed to Coldfoot. I envisioned it growing and becoming a real livelihood. I thought I was good for five years there and then I'd be able to sell. I developed enthusiasm for the place early on. I had been ready for a change in my life, and this was it.

I was in my glory being in this wilderness setting dealing with harsh conditions. I felt like a pioneer. This was why I came to Alaska. Other people had *talked* about doing this, but I was *doing* it. It helped that I had a wife who was 100 percent behind me, too. We worked our tails off. These were tough circumstances, but we made a success out of it.

I was happy when we got the long-term lease, but we had no money. I kept plowing all the revenue back into the operation, making improvements and thinking of ways to do better. BLM was interested primarily in the non-commercial traveling public, but I cared about the truckers.

Anyone who drives the Dalton Highway today would wonder what we were griping about. The road is so much better now. Twenty years ago it was barely fit to drive. The truckers driving semis finally protested the poor conditions by staging a mass "breakdown" twenty-eight miles north of Fairbanks at the end of the pavement. That got some attention. The state got some equipment out there and did more maintenance.

Still, the motoring public stayed away. A tourist told me that the Fairbanks visitors center had discouraged him from making the drive north, but that he came in spite of what they told him. He said they told him the road was horrible and, if he broke down, he'd be in the poor house before he got out.

On my next trip to Fairbanks, I dropped in at the visitors center to sniff around. I said, "I'm looking for something different to do. What's this Dalton Highway and driving up the Arctic Circle to Coldfoot?" I was told, "That's the last thing you want to do. Do you have four-wheel drive? You're at least going to get a broken windshield and you've got to carry extra gasoline and tires." The guy made a big deal out of it. I said, "Have you ever been up there?" He said no. So I said, "Then how do you know what you're talking about? It just so happens I own the facilities at Coldfoot. Lots of people drive up there and nothing goes wrong."

I went in to see the director and told her that they better change their attitude. I got the word later that they did.

It's true your car might take a beating on the Dalton Highway. Broken windshields and flat tires were common. We were fixing twenty or thirty truck tires a day. The Dalton wasn't for the faint of heart. You had to be adventuresome.

When I got the long-term lease, I needed money for development. It just so happened that Alyeska Pipeline Service Co. put up for sale some surplus camp buildings at Pump Station Five, thirty-eight miles south of Coldfoot. Alyeska offered a dozen eight-foot by fifty-foot bunkhouses, each with four rooms. I bid about $20,000. I had in mind to form these structures together as a motel. My bid was accepted, and I was given ten days to pay.

I drove to Wasilla for a conversation with my banker, who thought I was insane. But he had told me he would help me, so I threw down the blueprints and said, "Now's the time to do it." He looked up at Cathy and me and said, "What the hell are you trying to do up there, anyway?"

I did not pretend it was ever going to become the Taj Mahal. But I said some day the Coldfoot operation would be worth money. I reminded him that this wasn't your everyday truck stop. After listening a while, he leaned back in his chair, put his hands behind his head, and asked me how much it was going to take. I asked for $400,000. He said if the Small Business Administration went along, he would, too. The SBA gave me $270,000 to get started.

It was already June of the second summer, and we had a short construction season. I couldn't completely finish a lodge, restaurant, work shop, and housing in time for winter while bringing in fuel. I had only until August 1 to return the blue paddy wagon to Don Burt, too, so the restaurant was a priority. I had six weeks and not a stick of material on hand, but we served the first hamburger from our new kitchen at two a.m. the first day of August.

The motel had fifty-four beds with a lobby and an indoor toilet. Cathy took a picture of me using the toilet and called it "The first flush at Coldfoot."

Meanwhile, mail service was deplorable. Once a week a pilot brought mail into Wiseman. If the weather was bad we missed a week. I tried to rally the people in Wiseman to support improved service, but they viewed me as an outsider and didn't respond. So, I wrote Congressman Don Young and suggested Coldfoot needed better service.

Coldfoot was me, basically. I wanted my mail. But Don Young got behind us, and the U.S. Postal Service came through. They established Coldfoot Station. Cathy became the postmaster. The irony is that I was given a contract to deliver mail to Wiseman. Cathy got paid. I got paid.

The post office subcontracted to a new company to bring in the mail and lo and behold the plane from Fairbanks now stopped in Coldfoot. Then they decided it made more sense to have Lynden Trucking drop off mail three times a week. Once I delivered the mail to Wiseman by dog team, just to say that I did it. This made me feel like one of the old sled dog mail carriers from the early days.

The truckers appreciated what we were doing. We have a picture from the day we were erecting the eighteen-foot by thirty-six-foot front wall of the restaurant. Seventeen people are raising it, and about half of them are truckers.

Truckers helped us because Coldfoot became their place. Sometimes they even pounded nails. They brought us surplus stuff from Prudhoe Bay. We could call the dispatcher at any number of companies, tell them we were running short on eggs, and a driver would bring them.

Truckers heading north from Fairbanks burned one hundred gallons of fuel by the time they reached us. It was still 243 miles to Prudhoe Bay, and you bet they stopped to top off the tanks. They didn't dare go over Atigun Pass not knowing what the weather and road conditions would be.

Our being there helped them out. They could carry extra freight instead of extra fuel on the rig. That made them money. The entire time we sold diesel fuel, we kept the price the same as it was in Fairbanks. We made a profit, but certainly could have charged more. We did the volume, and I wasn't going to gouge the people who kept us going.

Coldfoot was unique. After Gov. Jay Hammond left office, he appeared in a TV series, "Jay Hammond's Alaska." He did an episode on us. On that show, I admitted that the prudent thing to do was to shut down for the winter, especially after the price of oil went down and Prudhoe Bay development slowed. But I wasn't going to do it. The truckers built Coldfoot, and I was going to accommodate them. They all knew it and they appreciated it.

From the time I arrived until the time I left, it was non-stop at Coldfoot. We were busy every waking moment. I went from being an Iditarod regular to an Iditarod no-show. I didn't train or race for years because I feared taking too much time off would be bad for the business.

I stayed involved with the board of directors, but missed meetings. Coldfoot wasn't more important to me than the Iditarod, but it demanded more. I still had some dogs left from the team, but for four or five years I rarely mushed.

Then, in 1986, Joe Redington got disgusted with his dog team in Nome and sold me the entire bunch of dogs for $20,000. Back then, it was the biggest dog deal of all time.

First mail delivery to "Coldfoot Station."

Dazzling the tourists

The tour company decided we needed a liquor license.
Only problem was we had gotten crosswise with the alcohol
control board doing a little bootlegging to miners in the area.

I gave a talk for tourists who came to Coldfoot on tours.

I HAD GROWN distant from the Iditarod, but it was not completely out of my life. I transacted board business mostly by phone. But we always went to Nome for the finish, and I emceed the banquets. But I didn't run the race and, after all my dogs were gone, that was it for a while.

Then, we reached a point at Coldfoot where we were free enough to take a vacation, and we wanted to spend it in Hawaii. Being warm took on new overtones.

Once we took off to Hawaii in January and when we returned we found out Coldfoot had experienced a freak thaw with temperatures rising as high as 32 degrees *above*! While we were gone the weather had been beautiful. As soon as we returned, the temperature dropped back to 40 and 50 below.

People asked, how we could live in such a place? Didn't we miss seeing people? I told them their assumption was wrong. We saw lots of people. Several hundred truckers passed through every day. They became a family, a community on wheels.

Over time the truckers watched us grow. And we shared their good times and bad times. Some got married and had children. Some graduated from school. Some got divorced. Some had accidents and got hurt. They became our friends, and some are friends to this day.

BLM didn't want Coldfoot to become a recognized community. The federal agency didn't want too many people there because Coldfoot sat on leased land, and it didn't want to have to make land available along the road corridor.

I was adamant that I would put the place on the map again, and not merely as a construction camp. That was my attitude. One thing that attracted visitors was the interpretive center put in by the BLM. And who supplied the electricity? We did. Ultimately, I bought my own telephone exchange and connected the state highway camp, the state trooper, the Alaska Department of Fish and Game guy, and the interpretive center. We had our own exchange—678.

In summer, we had close to thirty employees, in the winter about fourteen. In 1986, when the price of oil dropped, the traffic slowed to about fifty trucks a day. I was bemoaning our circumstances to a friend in Fairbanks, wondering how I would survive. And he had sensible advice. He suggested cutting back the operation to the minimum until we no longer were losing money and, when the economy improved, we could rev back up. If we didn't do this, we would be gone by the time the economy improved.

I went back to Coldfoot and announced we no longer would be open twenty-four hours a day. I told the employees they were welcome to stay and that we would feed them, but it might take us a while to get caught up on payroll. All but one stayed. We cut back to sixteen hours. We left out coffee, doughnuts, and pie on the honor system. Sometimes truckers woke us up if they needed fuel

One day, Tim McDonnell from Princess Tours stopped by and told us the company was considering starting some Dalton Highway tours and would need overnight lodging. He toured our fifty-four-bed, very Spartan facility and balked at the idea of using it because every room didn't have a bathroom. He said some clients wouldn't go for it. I told him I had the makings of a fifty-two-bed camp across the way and we could work with that.

McDonnell said that if I put a toilet and washbasin in every room it might work. I said, "If you've got the money, I've got the time." He looked at me and said, "Money's no problem."

We went to work in late summer 1986 in anticipation of the 1987 season. The deal was that Princess, which owns hotels all over Alaska and operates cruise ships, would bus people north along the Dalton Highway to Prudhoe Bay. The tours would overnight at Coldfoot. The tour people would fly them out of Prudhoe Bay, then load up a new group arriving by air and drive them south on the highway with another overnight stop at Coldfoot.

I brought my friend Roger Black back north to help. He was supposed to work for a month. He stayed four years. Through one of Cathy's brothers, we were referred to Brian Burroughs from Wisconsin, who was still at Coldfoot years later.

Burroughs had never seen mountains and he got an eyeful at Coldfoot, which sits in a beautiful valley in the foothills of the Brooks Range. One evening I saw Burroughs sitting outside on a log. I asked Cathy, what was the matter, was he unhappy? She guessed he was just looking at the mountains. I stopped to talk with him, and he said, "Isn't this place something?" His wife had traveled north from Wisconsin to find out when he was coming home, and he told her, "I am home." She left. He stayed.

Yet, Coldfoot wasn't for everyone. People stopped on those bus tours and told us what a great place it was, what an interesting life we had. But they wouldn't have lasted five minutes. It was fine as long as they were getting back on the bus.

We were working on the housing units and had installed twenty-six toilets and washbasins when Princess called and said this wasn't enough. They wanted showers, too. I told them it was going cost them. And it took some finagling to put it all into the space available, too.

Princess also decided it would be nice if we had a bar and liquor license. Only problem was that we had gotten crosswise with the state alcohol control board. We'd been doing a little bootlegging to miners in the area. We got caught, but the case was dismissed. Sure enough, the control board brought up this case in denying us a license.

I got an attorney. Six months and many thousands of dollars later, we had our liquor license. The trucking companies didn't like this. So I met with them and pointed out that the truckers were passing bars in Anchorage, Wasilla, Nenana, and Fairbanks. Coldfoot was no different. The truckers were adults.

Some of the drivers did come into the bar, had a couple of beers, spent the night, and then started out again the next day. Occasionally, a driver abused the opportunity, but we tried hard to control it. We had very few problems.

We did some good and had fun, too. A daughter of one of the mining families had cystic fibrosis and needed money for oxygen equipment. The truckers and the Alyeska pipeline people helped us bring in a band and put on a dance. We raised $3,000. Everybody came from all around. Truckers rearranged their schedules to be there. Miners crawled out of the woodwork.

We put together a trucker rodeo every year. They drove between flags in the parking lot. In 1984 we started the Coldfoot Classic, a 350-mile dog race above the Arctic Circle.

Every Thanksgiving and Christmas we invited everybody in the area to a turkey dinner buffet. Usually we served about one hundred people.

We sold a lot of fuel and food. Cathy made sure we maintained a $20,000 inventory of meat. Tourism expanded. Today independent travelers and smaller tour groups are important to Coldfoot. Smaller bus companies bring fifteen or so people at a time. These are the people who climb a mountain because it's there. They drive a road because it's there.

Really, Coldfoot was my true purpose for being in Alaska. But I was in the north for thirty years before I figured this out. Every day was a thrill at Coldfoot. I got up every morning ready to hit it and I hated to go to bed at night.

After a couple of years, I bought a semi and we hauled our own supplies from Fairbanks. I loved driving that road, especially on the home stretch cresting the top of Coldfoot Hill and looking into my valley.

In the summer, Coldfoot is the most beautiful place you could ever hope to be. In July 1988 the temperature reached 97 degrees above zero. The following January it hit 82 below. The summers are short but warm, with little wind. The first tour bus would show up the last weekend of May, and we would hope and pray the snow would be gone by then. It usually was.

The mountains are all around. If you stand in the parking lot and do a 360, you see hills and mountains in all directions. This is the northernmost part of the Rocky Mountains. Forty miles north of Coldfoot you come to Atigun Pass, which is more than four thousand feet above sea level. That's the highest point on the highway.

The elevation at Coldfoot is about one thousand feet. We were fifty miles south of the Arctic tree line, so we had lots of scrubby black spruce with some decent timber along the creeks and rivers. On the way to Atigun Pass you run out of trees. A marker points out the last tree you see heading north as you get into open tundra north of the pass.

Once I made the deal with Princess, I heard from Holland America. It wanted to start a tour, too, and more hotel rooms were needed. By then I knew what I was doing. Once again, I said, "If you've got the money, I've got the time." And they had the money. We built fifty-four more rooms in a new wing. This was a win-win deal. I owned the buildings, but Holland America funded the construction. I didn't need to make a capital investment. In the meantime, when the rooms weren't needed for tourists, I could rent rooms to the Alyeska work crews.

The first year, we saw fourteen buses the whole season—forty people per bus. In 1988, we averaged two buses per night from the end of May until September. We lodged three thousand people. The third year we had twice that number. We were open twenty-four hours a day, seven days a week. We never closed. We should have. We made our money in the summer and then ate it up in the winter. Cathy and I felt like we didn't get enough sleep for nine years.

At times all 108 beds were full, and drive-up tourists had to be put into the old motel. Most of these people had come north on cruise ships. This was the ultimate side trip.

Unfortunately, Princess promoted Coldfoot on my Iditarod reputation. It was fun at first. But this meant I had to be on hand whenever a bus came in. The tourists had been promised they would meet Dick Mackey, Iditarod champion. He'll tell you stories of the Iditarod, and so on. It got to the point where they expected me to climb on the bus and greet them. I gave the new arrivals a little speech and told them about dinner—a scrumptious buffet featuring prime rib and halibut. We hired good Alaskan chefs.

The next morning, before the tourists left, they spent an hour at the dog lot. They were excited to meet this Iditarod musher who lived in the middle of nowhere. I had a spiel that wouldn't quit. I jumped up on a wooden doghouse. I showed them the dogs—new dogs purchased from Joe—and the pups I was raising. I talked about how the Iditarod started, and my involvement with it, and how it had progressed. The tourists were like sponges. They soaked this stuff up.

Of course, they always asked what it took to survive at Coldfoot. I told them, first, you've got to be tough. And, second, you've got to be a little crazy. If you're both tough *and* crazy, you've got it made. By then, I had everybody chuckling.

I had three sleds in the yard. One was the remains of a sled. One was the sled I used in the first Iditarod. And one was new. The old sled had been sold in a Sears catalogue in about 1908. It had cast-iron fittings for the stanchions. I'd say ninety-eight percent of these visitors were sixty or older. Many had grown up on farms with outhouses and no electricity. They could identify with us.

The fancy meal we gave them didn't fit their image of Coldfoot. They were surprised to get more than a hamburger for dinner. We charged $14.50 for the meal and only once did I get a complaint about price. We served one thousand meals a day at Coldfoot.

At first, the truckers weren't happy to see the tourists on the road. But gradually they came to realize the tourists were their best allies for upgrading the quality of the road. Eventually, the Dalton Highway became a federal highway, and now the state receives ninety-five percent funding to maintain it.

The great part of Coldfoot's uniqueness was the national publicity. We got some free advertising that we couldn't have purchased for love or money. Princess and Holland America brought up travel writers and agents. We had full-page coverage in the *Orlando Sentinel* and the *Los Angeles Times*. Coldfoot had offbeat appeal.

We were America's farthest north truck stop.

How cold is COLD?

The northern lights were spectacular. A rainbow of colors danced from one end of the sky to the other, leaving us in awe. We never tired of seeing them.

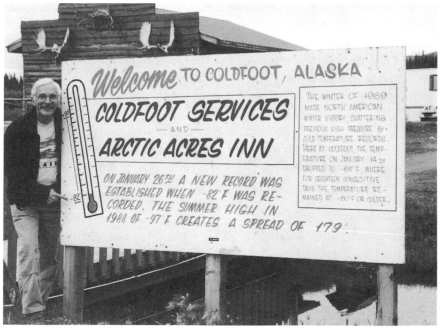

The temperature spread at Coldfoot was 179 degrees!

MINUS 82 DEGREES below zero.

The coldest temperature ever recorded in North America.

It was January 1989 when Coldfoot really earned its name. A film crew was staying with us while making a cold-weather commercial with musher Sonny Lindner for Craftsman tools. They brought with them six wolves that they had rented in Hollywood.

It was 56 degrees below the day they showed up. They went outside to take pictures of the thermometer. Their reaction was, "Wow! Look at this!" They didn't realize this would be the day's *high* temperature. The mercury kept dropping—60 below, then 65. For seventeen days, it never got warmer than 60 below and on January 26, the temperature bottomed out at 82 degrees below zero.

The Hollywood people were virtual prisoners at Coldfoot. It stopped being an adventure when the director froze his fingers. The temperature dropped so fast he and his crew couldn't get out. No planes were flying. This cold snap was so severe and widespread that it even shut down jet airports in Anchorage and Fairbanks for a few days.

Every day, the foreman at the state highway maintenance camp called in weather observations and temperature readings for the statewide weather report. On that day in January, the highest reading among three thermometers was 82 below, and that's what he reported.

I had heard that if the temperature dropped below minus 60 you couldn't feel the difference, as it got colder. Forget that! It was minus 60-something for two weeks before it dropped to 82 below, and we could feel a drastic difference.

We had twenty-seven oil-fired furnaces spread around the Coldfoot complex. Two of us took turns checking them twenty-four hours a day. You'd check one, and it was running fine. An hour later, the fuel had congealed and the furnace quit. We used torches to thaw the frozen fuel lines.

We had ten thousand gallons of propane underground. We siphoned it off into hundred-pound cylinders and brought them inside so we could keep the cook stoves going. We had six generators. Normally, two kept things running. During that cold stretch we needed four generators, and we were nervous about having only two in reserve. That kind of cold is tough on men and equipment. It was so cold that metal tools just shattered.

I wore insulated coveralls under my parka and two pair of gloves. I was lucky to have plenty of Arctic footwear. I was testing prototypes of new boots from the Timberland Company. Some believe no boot is good enough to keep your feet warm at those temperatures, but there is. The key is the liner. I wore a size ten boot, but in the cold I'd use a size twelve and put two insoles inside each boot. Halfway through the day, I took the bottom one out and put a new one on top. I made sure I had about an inch-and-a-quarter between the ground and me. I got cold feet, but never frostbitten feet.

Over the years, I did get a few frostbitten patches on my fingers and face. That was a fact of life if you were out in the cold all of the time. I don't know anybody from those days who didn't get some frostbite running the Iditarod.

Working in that cold is a mental drain. If I had been working at Prudhoe Bay I would have pulled up and gone home. But I was working for myself. I had to keep the place alive. There wasn't much time to think. Staying ahead of cold-weather problems took all our concentration. People depended on us.

When the temperature warmed to 60 below, it felt like a spring day. I remember running without a jacket the hundred or so feet to the shop. Cathy yelled at me for that. And when it warmed to minus 40, it was a heat wave!

We all talk about the cold weather and harsh environment, but I prefer to remember summer, when we had sunshine twenty-four hours a day. Seventy degrees was T-shirt weather. The fishing was terrific. One July, a dozen of us went to the south fork of the Koyukuk River and caught two hundred grayling in few hours. When you put a hook in the water, if you didn't bring out a fish it was because the hook had gotten caught in the rocks.

In the winter, there were twenty-two or so people around Coldfoot, counting the state workers and families, and about the same number down the road at Wiseman. But that isolation had its advantages. The northern lights at Coldfoot were amazing. No artificial lights interfered with your view. The lights are spectacular in a clear sky, the colors of the rainbow dancing night after night from one end of the sky to the other. You'd get up in the middle of the night, look out the window and go, "My God, look at this." We never tired of seeing them.

The worst thing that happened at Coldfoot was a fire in February during our second winter. I looked out the window, and the sky was ablaze. A gasoline-powered compressor had caught fire. The fuel tanks were situated between the shop and me and at first I thought they were going to blow. The parking lot was jammed with trucks. Our new fifty-ton wrecker was parked just outside the shop.

We took a heavy loss in that fire, and I didn't have a dime at the time. Alaska Marine in Anchorage gave us credit for a new air compressor. Three days later we were back in business.

Tire patching was our bread and butter. We charged forty dollars for a repair. The same work cost $125 at Prudhoe Bay. We worked on extra large, tube tires. Tubeless tires came later. It was not unusual for a trucker to blow half a dozen tires on a trip. One guy blew seventeen tires on a 1,000-mile round trip from Fairbanks to Prudhoe Bay. When he got back to Fairbanks, he was told, "Don't feel too bad. Twenty-one is the record."

We were a sketchy operation in the beginning. It took a while to get that first toilet running. We didn't have heat. A work crew had moved in, and the foreman sent a guy to Fairbanks to buy $3,500 worth of kerosene heaters for the rooms. I paid for them.

The biggest crisis was the 1986 oil shortage. The traffic slowed to a trickle. The trucking companies were charging $75,000 or $80,000 worth of fuel in a month. Suddenly, I started getting bankruptcy notices. I was left holding the bag for more than $300,000.

After I bought a semi, we drove to Fairbanks every week in the summer and every two weeks in the winter. In the city, we made twenty-five or thirty stops in one day. Our last year, we spent $187,000 on meat alone. In a single trip we might have twenty cases of eggs, six drums of oil, some lumber, some cement, and who knows what else.

In summer, the trip to Fairbanks took six hours, and it was an easier drive in the semi than in a car or pickup. The semi tires were so much larger they sailed over the ripples in the road. Back then there were no mileage markers. Eventually, the state marked prominent places on the highway. One of them was Mackey Hill. The story I heard was that it was named for a trucker who had lost control coming down the hill. I used to insinuate that Mackey Hill was named after me. This made Cathy cringe. "You can't be telling those stories," she said. I finally promised to stop.

Once we were giving a ride to a new gal coming to work and we passed the Mackey Hill sign. She asked if the hill was named after me. I could feel Cathy looking at me. I said no, and Cathy relaxed. Then I said, "Actually, it was named after my great-great-grandfather, who was the first Indian agent in the neighborhood."

Other places along the road had colorful names like Stormy, Connection Rock, Gobbler's Knob, and Beaver Slide. You had to know where you were every second. It's an intense road to drive in bad weather. There was nothing to make a tourist go out there in a snowstorm, but the truckers had to go.

On one trip, I was daydreaming when I hit the top of a place called Happy Man. It's a twenty-two percent grade with an "S" curve. I was going sixty mph fully loaded. Suddenly I realized where I was and knew I couldn't start downhill at that speed, so I just stuffed the whole semi into a snow bank. I had no choice. The next truck that came along hooked a chain onto me, and I came out fine. No big deal.

Cathy loved caring for her dogs—no easy task.

This wasn't named for me but I liked to say it was.

Bureaucrats and bears

Grizzlies were our greatest concern. Sometimes they came onto the porch and peered into the restaurant while people were eating. This was not a pleasant dining experience.

Late summer on the Dalton Highway in the Brooks Range.

Lew Freedman

WE WERE LIVING on the edge. Coldfoot was that kind of place. Much of the time we were winging it. We tried to get things done in a harsh environment using common sense. Occasionally our ways conflicted with the Bureau of Land Management. The BLM had rules, guidelines, whatever. Sometimes the government was flexible, sometimes it wasn't.

The first time an environmental inspection took place at a nearby pipeline pump station, an inspector stopped in at Coldfoot. He didn't like our outhouse. He didn't like us getting water from the slough. The guy said,

"Dick, I'm going to pretend I didn't stop." But he said, "I'll be back in a couple of months. I'd like to see some improvement." People worked with you most of the time.

Other times I fought tooth and nail over ridiculous things. Our landlord, the BLM, treated the pipeline corridor as if it was sacred ground.

I believed land allotments should be opened south of Atigun Pass to people who wanted to settle in the area. Why not allow people to build homes a quarter-mile from the highway? There would be no stampede. It takes a hardy breed to live there. What harm would it do? You've got the road. You've already got traffic. Big deal. Why not create a township with land for homes, a school, and a church?

We talked about making Coldfoot a township, but the idea fizzled. It was OK for BLM to grab all the land it wanted to build an interpretive center, or to build a fancy camp for government people, but God forbid that an ordinary person might have a nice place to live along a creek.

I fought restrictions the BLM wanted to impose on Coldfoot. My lease said I could have additional land if I could justify it as being beneficial to the business. It also said I could do anything on the land that was within the law.

Alyeska once operated a runway at Coldfoot, but when the pipeline-builders pulled out, they ran a furrow machine over the strip and reseeded it. It was unusable. Later, workers from Doyon, the Native corporation, came into the area repairing bridges. The crew ran a scraper over a gravel pit, put a roller on it, and soon we had a two-thousand-foot runway. Two-thirds of the strip was on my leased land; the rest was on federal land.

At one time, the original runway accommodated not only helicopter traffic for Alyeska but also planeloads of hunters. I have a picture of twenty-seven airplanes sitting on the runway. Then Alyeska gave up the old construction camp runway, less than a mile from our own airstrip. BLM said it was not allowed to be in the runway business. The state didn't want it because of the maintenance responsibility.

Anyway, I had myself an airstrip. I put in a sensor so that lights came on at night. At that point we had a runway, hotel, restaurant, service area, telephone exchange, and mail service. I practically invented a town. Of course, BLM said it couldn't permit me to have a runway. And when government officials came in to inspect it, where did they land? On my runway, of course.

BLM threatened me with a $10,000 fine for maintaining a runway. I said, "OK, I won't maintain it." We ripped out the lights. The strip didn't need maintenance. It became a Bush strip. The state trooper took off and landed there and said, "I don't see why I can't use it." Everybody knew it was a cheap shot by BLM.

Meanwhile, I had put in an extra entrance into the parking lot of the service station so the state's graders could come through without turning around when they were plowing snow. I did occasional plowing for the state when their graders were out the road. We worked together.

I was already supplying the state highway camp with telephones. Next I was going to supply the camp with power. We had a fine generation facility. We were open twenty-four hours a day. If something went wrong, a backup generator could be started. Just as we're about to sign a deal, somebody quashed it because we didn't have automatic switching gear. One of the state inspectors from Fairbanks asked, "What do you do if a generator goes down?" I said, "We start up another one."

Not long after, at about 40 below, one of the state generators shut down in the middle of the night. The generator was Alyeska surplus with fancy new switching gear. The automatic switching gear kicked in, and a few minutes later the second generator failed. The foreman came over, frantic. "Man, we're in trouble," he said. "It won't take long for things to freeze up." We unbolted one of our twelve-hundred-pound generators from its skids, unwired the whole thing and moved it to the state camp. The local people were grateful, but we didn't get a thank-you from the state people in Fairbanks. At Coldfoot, we all worked together regardless of what they said in town.

Then BLM got on my case for burning trash. The agency said I could burn regular trash, but not tires, nor anything toxic. I wanted a dump. The BLM wanted me to truck residue and whatever I couldn't burn to Fairbanks. I was told private citizens couldn't have a dump. Anyway, I burned my stuff for nine years and never hauled anything away. The residue just piled up. Eventually, BLM said I had to put a cyclone fence around it. That was another story.

I was told to build the fence to keep out the bears. A booklet of requirements was a half-inch thick. I had to have a six-foot cyclone fence. Protruding from the fence at exactly a forty-five-degree angle must be three strands of barbed wire with five points per barb. Another strand of barbed wire had to be six inches off the ground. There had to be insulators with five thousand volts of electricity. The head enforcement guy at the U.S. Fish and Wildlife Service didn't want me killing off bears. But what about people?

Trouble is, the Coldfoot parking lot was an open area. People could walk right up to an electrified fence. I went into the BLM office and told a woman overseeing this matter that I would build a fence to government specifications as long as she signed some papers first.

"What papers?" she asked.

"Absolving me from any responsibility if a tourist wanders up and falls against this fence."

"I can't do that," she said.

"Well, neither can I," I said. "Now we're back to square one. We're even. Goodbye." I never did build the fence.

An electrified fence would have fried some bears. Never mind people. There was a tremendous amount of wildlife in the Coldfoot area—wolves, moose, sheep, caribou, and bears. But our greatest concern was the grizzlies. Sometimes they came onto the porch and peered into the restaurant while people were eating. This was not a pleasant experience.

Grizzlies were less common than black bears, but we saw plenty of both. A state Fish and Game officer once counted seventeen grizzlies as he flew along the highway north of the Yukon River.

The bears were dangerous. Sometimes they had to be put down. Stepping out the door right into a black bear is unnerving. The worst thing was when people stepped off the tour buses and walked into the brush trying to get pictures. It didn't matter if you warned them. Some people never listen. We were horrified to think what could happen.

Once, a guest opened a back door at the motel, and there was a grizzly. About thirty people rushed outside to see it. Nervous, the bear retreated 150 feet into the bushes. Three people followed it with cameras. Cathy and some other employees yelled at them to stay back.

Soon these people, a man and two women, were in brush over their head. I jumped into my truck and zipped over to Fish and Game. I wasn't about to go in after them. The Fish and Game guy said, "I hope they make it. I'm not going in there, either."

Luckily, nobody got hurt.

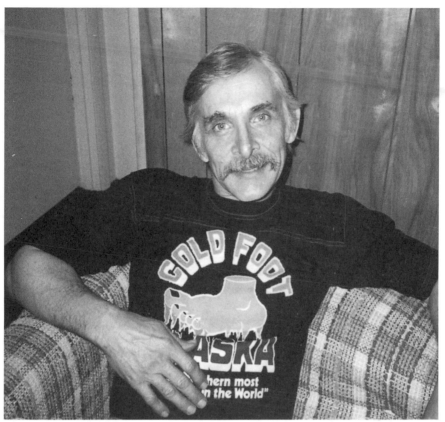

Our logo? A drawing of a frozen foot, of course.

The Coldfoot **24** Classic

We had a mass start for the Coldfoot Classic.
Everybody was inside sleeping bags, dogs unharnessed,
when we fired a starting gun. The news media loved it.

A scene from the starting line of the Coldfoot Classic.
.

THE ALL-TIME most popular Coldfoot souvenir was our signature T-shirt. On the front was a drawing of a foot dripping with icicles, done by Bill Devine, the artist who designed so much merchandise for the Iditarod.

That first summer, I stopped in to see Bill when I went back to Anchorage on Iditarod business. He said, "Coldfoot? You've got to have a logo." He liked the name. He took out a scratch pad and drew a cold foot in a few minutes, and that was it. I put that picture on a sign at the entry to the parking lot. I put it on the stationery. It was everywhere.

Part of the deal when we sold the place was that we had to release the logo to the new owners. Later, when Cathy and I began traveling, we saw Coldfoot items all over. We ran into a guy in Italy wearing a Coldfoot cap. I asked where he got it and he said, "I was there." I said, "Funny thing, so was I."

The logo helped establish Coldfoot. We also designed Coldfoot souvenirs for special occasions and "Coldfoot, the northernmost truck stop." We sold tens of thousands of T-shirts.

About 1985, there was a problem on the pipeline at Dietrich Camp, thirty-five miles north. The pipeline had sagged where it was buried in an old riverbed, and Alyeska Pipeline Service Co. had to make repairs. One of the surveyors, a regular visitor, stopped by and told us to get ready for an influx of workers. All we had to offer at the time was fifty-four beds in the old motel.

An Alyeska helicopter landed an hour later. Three top-echelon guys wearing white hats came in and inquired how many beds we had, and were they rented? "Not at this moment, but they could be by this evening," I said. He said, "We have a little problem on the pipeline. We'll rent all fifty-four beds." He said sixty-five people would be coming and going.

Alyeska wanted to pay once every ninety days, but I insisted they pay weekly. Their people stayed with us for six weeks and this put us on the road to financial stability.

Of course, we created a T-shirt to commemorate the event. A cartoon-like scene showed band-aids on the pipeline with oil spurting out. I was worried Alyeska—my benefactors—would be offended, but the Alyeska people bought hundreds of them. I ordered one thousand T-shirts, and I thought committing to that many was a risk. We sold nearly ten thousand of them.

Some of the crew was dissatisfied with the accommodations, and some minor vandalism took place. My people were afraid I would jeopardize the one hundred dollars per night, per room that Alyeska was paying, but I told the union steward for the pipeliners that his men had to calm down or they could clear out.

Counting fuel purchases, I pulled in $8,000 to $10,000 a day. The amazing thing is that the $50,000 buy-out payment to Don Burt was due soon, and Cathy was beside herself worrying how we would pay him. When the time came, we had the money.

For the first time in years, I was far removed from dog racing and the Iditarod, so I decided to promote Coldfoot and get a mushing fix by organizing a new race—the Coldfoot Classic. In the early 1980s, I still had a few aging veterans from my 1978 championship dog team. We also had four-dozen puppies that Cathy was raising. Cathy worked ten hours a day and then spent five or six hours with the puppies. Brian Burroughs, who worked for me, and my son, Bill, who lived in Wiseman, also had dogs. So we put on a 350-mile race in April 1984 that started and ended in the parking lot of Coldfoot Services.

The Coldfoot Classic became another of my adventures with the government, this time mostly with the National Park Service. We needed a permit to run through the Gates of the Arctic National Park. Right away the Park Service said no.

I pointed out that the Alaska National Interest Lands Conservation Act guaranteed the right to travel between communities. An organized race was not the intent, they said. I said, "Quite often you make rules that don't seem to have the intent you start with. I could invite five thousand snowmachiners from New York and take a trip through Anaktuvuk Pass."

I wheeled and dealed and stomped my feet and raised a fit. Finally, they agreed I could have a race, but with no more than thirty mushers. I couldn't offer a cash purse, only prizes. And I couldn't put in a trail using anything but a dog team—no motorized vehicles. There was great interest when word got out we were having a dog race completely above the Arctic Circle.

Our costs for the race were about $10,000. I tried to keep down the costs for the mushers because I knew it would be expensive for them to get to Coldfoot. They would be able to stay in the Coldfoot motel for next to nothing.

The race was run the first week of April from Coldfoot to Wiseman to Anaktuvuk Pass to Bettles and back to Coldfoot. It was the last race of the season. We did some funky things to make it fun, including a mass start. Everybody was inside sleeping bags, the dogs unharnessed, when we fired a signal gun. The mushers jumped out of the bags, hooked up the dogs, and took off. It was as if someone had set off a gold stampede. It was fun to watch, and the news media loved it.

In Anaktuvuk Pass, which had never seen racing dog teams come through, people turned out to watch in their finest furs. They came from all around on snowmachines. When the leader, Lavon Barve, approached the village, people began calling the dogs. What a spectacle!

It was 40 degrees above zero at the start. That evening, over at the north fork of the Koyukuk River, it was 45 below with a howling wind. What a transformation, but that's Alaska.

And who won the first race? Rick Mackey. First prize was a snowmachine. We had a good cast of mushers. My son Bill ran, too, as did Ron Aldrich and Charlie Boulding.

Charlie is a top Iditarod musher now and has won the Yukon Quest twice. This was his first race, and he won't ever forget it. Leaving the north fork he was climbing a steep slope glaciated with polished ice. He took off his parka because he was sweating so badly, and suddenly the dogs got away from him and turned around. It was dark and he slept in a snow bank without a coat at forty below. The next morning he found his team—and coat—about one hundred feet away. The dogs hadn't made a sound, and Charlie was lucky to be alive.

In 1985, Susan Butcher won the classic. She had been a favorite in the Iditarod the previous month, but her team was stomped by a moose, and she had to drop out. So her team was trained and fresh. That was the year that Libby Riddles became the first woman to win the Iditarod, attracting international attention. If any finish superseded my one-second victory over Swenson, Libby's was the one.

Soon enough, Susan began winning the Iditarod. She saw herself as a dog musher, not a *female* dog musher. Still, women's groups celebrated her successes, and this did her no harm. Susan won four times in five years. Libby was the initial recipient of all the attention, though. After Libby won, the Women's Sports Foundation named her the U.S. women's athlete of the year, and to this day she has done well because of her incredible victory. Libby is credited with the surge of interest in the Iditarod among women, though Susan later became better known among fans.

By its second year, the Coldfoot Classic was getting grief from the Wilderness Society. The organization tried to get an injunction to stop the race because it was going through a national park. The BLM opposed the race, too. But the general public, the newspapers, the people of Anaktuvuk Pass, and the North Slope Borough all supported the race. I was a thorn in the park service's side.

The Wilderness Society brought Susan Alexander in from Washington, D.C. She let me know she was going to stop the race and came to Coldfoot to confront me. I wined and dined and wooed her. I suggested we lessen the race's impact on the park by having a restart at Anaktuvuk Pass. I convinced her that the mushers would simply enjoy the park on their way to the restart. Of course, the mushers blasted out of Coldfoot as fast as they could because the earlier they got to Anaktuvuk, the more rest they and their dogs would have.

After I schmoozed her, we were standing by the cash register in the restaurant and I said, "You know, Susan, this hasn't been all that bad. You're not near the bitch I thought you were when you got here." She laughed and took it.

The third year, Joe Runyan won. He's also won the Yukon Quest and the Iditarod. The fourth year Jeff King won. He has won the Quest and the Iditarod three times. First-class bunch, huh?

In 1987, we took a year off because I went back to the Iditarod. Then we held the Coldfoot Classic one more time in 1988, and King won again. By 1989, I was ill, and Cathy and I decided to sell out.

The 1986 race was special because I competed in my own race. I had bought that dog team from Joe Redington in Nome and raced it a month later. I was second behind Rick heading into Anaktuvuk Pass. Things were going well until I came out of there and got onto mile after mile of glare ice. Boy, those dogs hated ice. I fell back, finishing fifth. I had a great time, though.

Rick Swenson ran that year, too, and he said, "That's some of the most beautiful country I've ever been in. I can't compare it to anything else. I've run on every kind of trail there is here—all of it bad. If the Iditarod was like this, no one would ever complete it."

We had so many government hassles. When the Gates of the Arctic National Park was created, the National Park Service confiscated a lot of homesteads and cabins in the Bettles area, and the people there had a grudge against the government. One of the complaints from the Wilderness Society was that the dogs would poop and their feces would blend into the terrain and introduce new grain, oats, and wheat. I had to go to the state agriculture agency for proof this would not occur. Everybody had a good laugh about this. The second year, the people in Bettles made up little packages for each musher containing diapers to put on the dogs. It was their way of ridiculing the park service and the Wilderness Society.

The park service was also upset because I had drawn attention to an old winter trail that came off the Yukon River. It was a traditional trail used for trapping, and we reopened it three feet wide. It hadn't been used for more than half a century.

The park service said we couldn't cut a trail. I pulled out the map that read "Winter Sled Dog Trail, Department of the Interior." This meant that our right to use the trail was protected under the same federal law that led to creation of the park.

I said, "That's the trail we're using." They said, "We don't recognize that." I said, "Excuse me, isn't the park service part of the Department of the Interior?"

Guess what, that trail no longer is included on park service maps.

Racing to Nome again

During my last Iditarod race, a vet told me he suspected my dogs had heat stroke. I said, "Heat stroke? Whoever heard of getting heat stroke in the winter?"

I hugged son Rick after he won the 1983 Iditarod.

THE 1983 IDITAROD gave me one of my greatest mushing thrills, and I wasn't even in the race. That was the year that my son Rick won.

Until that year, Rick had been up and down. He had scratched a couple of times. He was eleventh in 1982. He was still finding his way in the race.

Rick even had problems the year he won. He and a couple of other mushers got off the trail between Grayling and Kaltag. That ticked him off, and he adopted an "I'll show you" attitude. He fought his way back to the front.

He had come to the starting line with optimism and then drew bib number thirteen. That's the same number I wore the year I won. He was charged up and ready to go. Thirteen was also the number Emmitt Peters wore when he won. Thirteen is a lucky number in the Iditarod.

Rick was running in front when he and some others got off on a trap line trail. The weather was bad, and they couldn't see where they were going. So, when they came into the stretch at White Mountain, about eighty miles from Nome, Eep Anderson had a two-hour lead.

I was sitting in the Polar Bar in Nome waiting when Peter Henning and his film crew came in from the trail to get more film, having landed in a helicopter on the sea ice. Peter told me he had spotted Rick at Topkok, and that Rick had closed to within twenty minutes of Eep. He invited me to join him for another look.

I was so pumped up that I ran right out and jumped into the helicopter without my parka. I just about froze to death. We flew back down the trail and spotted Eep. Then we landed, and here came Rick. I told him he was closing in on the lead. He looked like a zombie. Later, at Safety, twenty-two miles from the finish, I saw Rick again and this time he was only thirteen minutes behind Eep. Good old thirteen. Rick was on a dead run. He signed into the checkpoint and was gone.

We flew around, Peter's crew shot some film, and when we started back toward Nome we couldn't find the teams. Then, at Cape Nome, ten miles from the finish, we finally spotted a headlamp. At first I thought it was Eep, but it wasn't. Rick had taken the lead. He was moving fast, but kept looking over his shoulder all the way to Front Street. As it turned out, he was adding distance then. Eep just crashed, and Rick beat him by an hour and forty minutes.

When we landed in Nome, I found Cathy and Rick's wife, Patti, and gushed, "You won't believe it! Rick's going to win this thing!" And he did. I was ecstatic. If Rick has a bad back today, it's from me thumping on it that day. Him winning was as good as me winning. That was something, I'll tell you.

We went over to the Bering Sea Saloon to celebrate, and it was quite a scene. Rick was wringing wet with sweat, disheveled, and exhausted. He said, "I just can't believe I did it, dad."

People still talk about us as the only father and son to win, even after all these years. Fathers and sons have run since then, but not both won. Tim Osmar, who has been near the front for years, may be the best bet to join his father Dean, who won in 1984.

I was excited, too, when my son Bill entered in 1984. Rick's championship had given Bill enthusiasm. Bill had never been much for competition.

He loves mushing, but he'd just as soon camp as race. He doesn't have the killer instinct for competition.

Bill ran junior races from the get-go and competed in the Coldfoot Classic, but his only Iditarod run was in 1984. Bill was a good dog trainer. He had a leader he could steer like a truck. But he had to drop that dog, and the race became a struggle after that. Even without a leader, he kept going. He thought about scratching at Elim, but went on to win the red lantern and $500. He overcame adversity, and I was so proud of him when he crossed under the arch in Nome.

Dogs are Rick's livelihood. He races every year. He sells dogs. His longevity is impressive. Of all of the mushers who started out around 1975, only he and Rick Swenson were adaptable enough to change with the times and new technology and stay near the front. He's a hell of a dog man.

In the mid-1990s, Rick moved over to the Yukon Quest, the second biggest long-distance race in the world. The distances between Quest checkpoints are longer than in the Iditarod. You are limited to one sled so, if you break it, you'd better be prepared to repair it. At Dawson City, the halfway point, you have a thirty-six-hour layover. The international race offers a smaller purse. All that makes the Quest different from the Iditarod.

For three years, Rick ran the Quest, finishing second, first, and third. He won in 1997.

Back in the 1970s and 1980s, Rick and I conferred often about mushing. The Iditarod is a different race now, much faster, and he doesn't ask my advice much. Rick is his own man now. But we do talk strategy, and he respects my input. What was a good dog twenty years ago is still a good dog.

I'd love to be the one mushing down Fourth Avenue on my way to Nome—that is, until the first day's racing ended, and I was looking for a warm bed and looking for my wife to fix me a hot meal.

I'm tickled watching Rick race and seeing him happy with his high finishes. And I take satisfaction in knowing Bill is regarded as a top mushing guide in the Arctic. He has a tremendous reputation and is successful. I wouldn't enjoy giving tours in the Arctic cold. As I got older, I found that heat feels good on your old joints. I had reached my limit on cold.

But in 1987, I hadn't reached that point. I had a fresh dog team, courtesy of Joe Redington, and I entered the Iditarod again. Rick took a look at my team said he and thought I could win again.

I had been race manager in 1981, and everything went smoothly. So I agreed to take the job again 1985, but that race was bedeviled by weather—storm after storm pounded the trail. That was the year Libby Riddles won by running into a fierce storm while others waited it out.

We had new trailbreakers out of Rainy Pass, and the trail wasn't put in where it always had been. The leaders had to turn around. I was elsewhere along the trail at the time. We had an inexperienced race marshal, bad weather, and a new trail. The combination of disagreements, trouble getting supplies to the checkpoints, and the weather shut down the race a couple of times. I was furious. You don't shut down the Iditarod, you tough it out. My ego was hurt, and I felt wounded. I was crucified by the Iditarod committee, by nearly everyone, for not having supplies in position.

It didn't matter that the weather was horrendous, and planes couldn't fly. It had been my obligation to see that the supplies were in the checkpoints, and they weren't there. *If you take the seat, you take the heat.* At the time, unfortunately, I blamed the weather. All this contributed to having the slowest race in years. I was wrung out at the end.

That was the end of my career as Iditarod race manager, but certainly not my interest in the Iditarod. So, in 1987, I decided to run again. From the start, training was difficult because of the workload at Coldfoot. But I worked it out. I trained during the day, at night, whenever I had time. Rick was living at Coldfoot and training there, too.

My longest training runs were eighty miles. Sometimes daughter Kris came with me, and sometimes my granddaughter Brenda came. We mushed out in the cold, made a bonfire, stayed for an hour or two, and then turned around. It got pretty nippy.

My dogs seemed to peak in training. They were veterans, and they were the right age. I thought this team could do something. The day we left Coldfoot it was 55 below. It had been steady at 40 below or colder for a couple of months. That was the dogs' environment. When we got to Anchorage a week before the race, it was 43 degrees above zero. And the temperature stayed above zero.

This was much too warm for my dogs. But they had a week to acclimate, and when I took them to the Tudor Track for a workout, they seemed fine. I wasn't too worried.

The first day of the Iditarod, I let them run. They weren't pushing hard. They seemed comfortable. The second day, dogs were dropping like flies. They were sick. I didn't know why. By the time I reached Nikolai, 350 miles into the race, I had dropped half a dozen dogs. And Rick's race wasn't going well, either.

Halfway to Nome, I was in the middle of the pack. The temperature was dropping, and my dogs perked up a little. But when we reached Ophir, a vet looked over my dogs and told me he suspected they'd had heat stroke. I said, "Heat stroke? Whoever heard of getting heat stroke in Alaska in the winter?" Another vet reached the same conclusion. Going from the extreme cold of Coldfoot to warmer weather was my downfall.

I did the best I could. But the dogs were sapped of energy by the time we climbed into the hills between Iditarod and Shageluk. I stopped by the trail, built a fire, and here came Rick. His dogs were listless. We sat around drinking coffee and talked, then backtracked fifteen miles to Iditarod and rested some more.

Along came Joe Redington, discouraged and ready to quit. But I wouldn't let him. And he wouldn't let me. We ran together, fed off each other, and had a good time. We camped, drank coffee, told stories. It was like a reunion. We spent a long time talking about how far behind we were.

Rick was forced to scratch, but Joe and I went on together. I was thirty-second and Joe was thirty-third. He came into Nome disgusted and said he was never going to race again. Not me. I said I would be back the next year.

As it turned out, Joe kept racing. He was eighty when he ran the Iditarod the last time. I was the one who never ran again.

We were overwhelmed by the business. I had no time to take care of the dogs, let alone train. So I decided to divest. Some dogs went to Rick and Bill, and some I sold. I remember the last time I gave a talk to the tourists at the dog lot. For the first time in almost thirty-five years I didn't have any racing dogs. At one time we had 150.

The next day Bill took the last thirty dogs back to Bettles. It was a sad day, and I cried.

Celebrating our democracy

When we were in Washington, D.C. for President Reagan's inauguration, someone stole three of Joe's dogs. The national news media picked up the story, and the FBI investigated.

Can you believe this picture of Joe and me?
Bill Devine

IN JANUARY 1981, I joined Joe Redington, Herbie Nayokpuk, and Norman Vaughan as a handler when they brought a team of Alaska sled dogs to Washington, D.C. for the inauguration of President Reagan.

Don Montgomery, who also had raced the Iditarod, helped coordinate our visit on that end and found us a place to stay. Joe, Herbie, and Norman were to be in the parade. Joe invited me to come along.

It was a memorable experience being with the other Alaskans in the inaugural parade. Others on hand were Al Crane, another former Iditarod president; Jan Masek; and, of course, Vi Redington. We had a good contingent of Alaskans.

Most of the Alaskans flew commercially to Washington, but I accompanied the dogs on a Boeing 747 Flying Tigers freighter. The airline's senior pilot was in command. He had been with Flying Tigers for decades, had even flown with Claire Chennault in China during World War II.

I asked the pilot and co-pilot all kinds of questions as we loaded the dogs. I was curious about the Flying Tigers, and the crew was curious about the dogs. Then it came out that I flew my own plane, a Cessna 180, so there was a lot of blah, blah, blah after that. By the time we got off the ground in Anchorage we were discussing tonnage, payloads, and airplane capabilities.

After we had been in the air a few hours, the co-pilot announced he was headed back to the galley to make some lunch and asked the captain if it would be OK if I slipped into his seat. No problem. The captain showed me the systems and talked about the plane's limits. He said, "It's no different than your 180. Here, let me take it off auto pilot and you can get a feel for it."

For about ten minutes, I flew a 747. It was awesome. The pilot coached me to make subtle directional shifts, warning me not to do anything drastic. I was elated, and for me this set a positive tone for the whole trip.

When we Alaskans joined up for the inaugural, we were excited to be part of something big. It didn't matter what your party affiliation was, you felt patriotic seeing democracy at work.

Norman and I stayed in the same hotel. Norman was a military man—everyone knows him as Colonel Vaughan—and he had a lot of old friends at the Pentagon. We visited his admiral and general buddies. Some had been his classmates at Harvard. Of course, Norman never graduated. He dropped out to accompany Admiral Richard Byrd to Antarctica in 1928, turning his back on a military or business career to embark on a life of adventure.

The generals and admirals were retired, but still had offices and staff and lots of stars on their shoulders. All of them wanted to talk about Norman racing in the Iditarod.

The Alaskans were a big hit. One night, we all were invited to an elegant home with cut-glass goblets and that sort of thing. Afterward, as we strolled on a long walkway next to a manicured lawn on a beautiful, moonlit night, Herbie and his wife, Elizabeth, disappeared. They had been a few steps behind. There they were, stopped back on the walkway, looking up at the moon. I laughed and said, "Gee, Herbie, haven't you ever seen the moon before?" He replied, "Not that high in the sky."

Later, at one of the inaugural balls, the men wore tuxedos. Someone joked that a picture of us grubby mushers all wearing tuxedos could be used for blackmail. We met Charlton Heston. That was like saying hello to Moses. I happened to get into a conversation with a senator's wife, who said, "Oh, you're from Alaska." She said it like, "You're from outer space." She asked questions that demonstrated a complete ignorance of Alaska. I hoped her husband wasn't as ignorant as she was.

Then, someone stole three of Joe's dogs from the suburban farm where he was staying. Joe's great leader, Feats, was one of them. This created an uproar when the national news media picked up the story. The FBI even got involved. Things were tense for a couple of days. It turned out that a couple of teenagers took the dogs. One of their mothers heard something on the radio and told the police she thought one of the missing dogs was in her basement.

The parade route was two miles long. President Reagan was into horses, and boy, there were plenty of horses in the parade. I have never seen anything like it. Bands represented every conceivable form of music in the country. Every military branch was represented, as was every state and territory. The first mile was a warm-up before we reached the reviewing stand. If a horse acted up, it was pulled out of line, and the ranks were closed. Everything was to be perfectly orchestrated as we turned onto Pennsylvania Avenue.

Our three-dog teams were supposed to remain twenty feet apart. I don't mean nineteen and I don't mean twenty-one. They wanted precision. This was a challenge. Thousands of people lined the parade route, making the dogs a little edgy. They were full of energy and tried to pull away, digging their claws in the pavement. But we managed to keep them in line. We certainly didn't want a dog team yanked from the parade for misbehaving.

The temperature was above freezing—too warm for the dogs. And we were hot, too, decked out in parkas, mukluks, and fur hats. We were wringing wet.

In the reviewing stand were President Reagan, Vice-president George Bush, the entire Supreme Court, and several hundred other dignitaries. We had been told not to hesitate. Keep moving. We could acknowledge the President with a slight bow of the head, but under no circumstances were we to *wave.*

When Reagan saw our rather outlandish delegation, he turned to Bush and appeared to ask, "Who's this?" Screw the rules. We waved.

We were at the swearing-in ceremony, too. I remember at one point Al Crane and I looked at one another, both of us surprised by how emotional we had become.

A lifetime supply of boots

The team raced down the bumpy trail like a runaway freight train. At the bottom, the director had a better idea what it took to handle eighteen energetic sled dogs.

Sons Rick and Bill at a fall hunting camp.

CERTAIN PARTS of your body—face, hands, and feet—are harder to protect than others in extreme cold. You need the right gear.

In the mid-1980s, Timberland was a little shoe company in Portsmouth, New Hampshire that decided to use Alaska as a testing ground for their boots. Owned by two brothers, it was not a well-known company until it spent a lot of money on national advertising. Timberland approached the Iditarod about a testing program, and someone recommended that they get in touch with me in Coldfoot.

Timberland's earliest boots were terrible. I mean it. It was a rubber, layered boot that split apart in cold weather. I will give them credit, though. I was put in direct communication with the guy in charge of research and development, and I discovered the company was willing to make changes on practically a daily basis to make a better boot.

They contacted me because I lived in the coldest place in North America, and because I was well known because of my connection to the Iditarod. There was no mention of any remuneration, but I got all of the boots I wanted. Next thing I knew, they asked if I would help make a commercial.

The company flew some dogs and me by helicopter to a glacier not far from Anchorage. It was an extensive shoot, and gratifying financially—big money. And it was fun. But the filming was exceedingly difficult because the director had no idea about the ability or limitations of a dog team.

The purpose of the commercial was to show off the toughness of the boots, that you could wear them in the cold, even while mushing a dog team. And that they were waterproof. I proved that. Boy did I ever. The dogs and I went through water for hours. Finally, I said, "One more time, and that's it." We had been there for two weeks for one sixty-second commercial.

I discovered that if you let them, directors would make you jump off a cliff to get what they want. This was a first for me. I was willing and cooperative, but there were limits.

I didn't have a speaking part. I just ran the dogs. One scene called for me to mush up the side of a hill and essentially fall off a cliff. It was straight down. The dogs had to be running. Give me a break. I was willing to go up the hill, but there was a two-thousand-foot drop just beyond the edge on the other side. I tried to bargain with him. It did no good.

I had been sweating bullets for days about this scene. I was losing sleep over it. And when I did sleep, I had nightmares. I wanted to satisfy the director, but I could see no safe way to do what he wanted. I finally said, "I'm not going do it." He just said, "OK." No argument. No show of disgust. Nothing. That was a lesson learned about directors.

We had gone way up on this glacier to film. Our camp was set up down below and, to return to camp, we had to follow a rough trail. Although it wasn't smooth, it was solid enough trail to support the dogs, and that was the best thing that could be said for it.

During filming, we would hang around for two hours, then work for five minutes. The dogs were charged up every time. They got bored with the repetition, but never physically tired.

One day, after shooting, I asked the director if he wanted to ride in the sled back to camp. I could barely keep a straight face. I hooked up those energetic dogs and let them run. They raced down that trail like a runaway freight train. We hit the bumps pretty hard, and our passenger bounced up and down wildly, wide-eyed, grabbing at air. By the time we got to the bottom of the hill, the director had a different perception of what it took to handle eighteen dogs.

After that, he was more reasonable, as in "Here's what I'd like to do. Can you do that? Is that OK?"

The commercial ran for sixteen weeks during the college football season. Later, my son Rick and I made another commercial for Timberland at Prudhoe Bay. We made a third commercial at Hatcher Pass.

In December 1986, I was invited to speak at Timberland's annual sales meeting in Fort Myers, Florida. Four hundred people from all over the world were there. My directive was to relate the Iditarod to their work. I was supposed to compare the superhuman effort of running the Iditarod with the superhuman effort they put into selling the company's products.

I began by comparing the weather in Florida with the weather in Coldfoot.

"These past several days have been an eye-opener for me and Cathy," I said. "It was quite a discovery to find out that all water does not freeze in the winter. And it's quite enjoyable to see women walking around in silky dresses and bathing suits, especially if they have nice legs. You can actually *see* women's legs here!"

Some guy hollered, "Careful, Dick, your wife is here." And I shot back, "Hell, I found out she's got legs, too." The place erupted, and I had them in the palm of my hand.

I told them their boots had held up under the toughest challenge—racing the Iditarod—and that if there were weaknesses in the boots, somebody could get hurt badly. But I assured them there were no weaknesses.

Also I made a connection between Timberland boots and the cold. I told them it had been my goal to win the Iditarod. "It's no different than the goals you have. When you succeed, you're successful. Winning the Iditarod is the same as succeeding at your sales goal. If you ask yourself why you do it, recognition from your peers has a lot to do with it. In our society, financial remuneration is a necessity, too. But when you stop to think about why you're successful, you realize it's something that comes from within. I'm not used to getting up in front of a group of people such as yourselves who are not sled dog-oriented, but right now I have a sense that you are people who have that inner drive for success."

Timberland was the major Iditarod sponsor for years. I maintained a relationship with the company even after I left Coldfoot. They were good for me. I still have Timberland boots. Those are the only boots I wear because I have a lifetime supply of them. I don't mean a lifetime *supplier*. I mean a lifetime supply, because they last so long. I've even given away boots.

I was sorry when Timberland split up with the Iditarod, but not surprised. Animal-rights activists generated a lot of heat, and Timberland became sensitive to the complaints. That's a shame, but the company had grown so big it didn't need the Iditarod anymore.

Timberland's tie to the Iditarod was a business proposition, and it had achieved its goals

Nine years **28** was enough

Driving back to Coldfoot for the first time since my illness, I despised what I saw. As much as I loved it, my life was more important than the business.

America's farthest north truck stop in fall 1984.

COLDFOOT was so demanding, it wore me out. I always thought of myself as invincible. That's my nature. What's wrong with twenty hours a day on a dead run? I used to do it, why can't I keep it up? I used to smoke and drink, too. I gave up drinking, smoking, working hard.

Changing jobs and careers, I'd walked away from several retirements during my working life. Coldfoot ended up being my retirement.

I don't know how long we would have stayed in Coldfoot if I hadn't become ill. My body was absolutely fatigued. I didn't realize I had been courting illness for some time, and what a jerk I became because of this fatigue. It helped that I had an understanding wife.

I kept an airplane at Coldfoot for use in an emergency. The first real emergency was mine, and I was in no shape to fly the plane. I suffered a physical meltdown in the summer of 1989. I was fifty-six. Cathy chartered an airplane to fly me to the hospital in Fairbanks. I was in intensive care for a week, but the doctors couldn't figure out what was wrong.

So I went back to Coldfoot and was gung-go again. We were building another hotel wing for Holland America, and my attitude was, "See, there was nothing wrong with me." Then I keeled over. It was August 14, 1989. I had been watching TV when I fell from a chair to the floor.

Cathy ran across the road to get the state Fish and Game officer, who was a medic. The consensus was that I wasn't going to make it. They figured it was my heart. My blood pressure had soared.

It didn't help the situation that the weather was horrendous—pouring rain, thunderstorms, and darkness. Andy Greenblatt, a friend who lived in Bettles, flew over in his Cherokee 6. Nobody should have been flying that night, but good old Andy did. While we waited, they put me on a stretcher and gave me oxygen from a tank we had in the repair shop.

Andy loaded Cathy, the medic, and me into his plane and flew us to Fairbanks. I was rational and awake. In the excitement, Andy forgot to switch fuel tanks, so the engine quit as we got to the Yukon River. It took about ten seconds to switch tanks, and in the meantime we were spiraling down in this awful storm. Lying there, I said, "What are you trying to do, Andy, kill us all?"

Before all this happened, I had made an appointment to see a heart specialist in Seattle. When we arrived in Fairbanks, our doctor arranged with Alaska Airlines to get me flown to Seattle on a stretcher with monitors.

By the time we reached Seattle I felt better and made jokes about the driving as the ambulance took me to Swedish Hospital. The doctors there ran tests and decided there was nothing wrong with my heart. That was the good news. The bad news was they did not know what was wrong. I stayed there two weeks for more tests. Seven doctors checked me out. I had no insurance.

Right away, the guy in charge, Dr. Peterson, threatened me about smoking. I was smoking a pack a day and had been a smoker for more than thirty years. "You have smoked your last cigarette," he said. "I'm a busy man, and you're a grown man. You don't want me following you around, and I don't have the time to follow you around. But I promise

This was our first "big rig" for trucking in supplies.

you that if you continue to smoke, someone else is going to enjoy the fruits of your labor."

That got my attention. It had more impact on me than being told I might get lung cancer. The doctors held a conference with me and said they couldn't pinpoint specific problems, but they felt I was working too hard, built up too much stress, and no longer could keep up the pace.

I came up with a solution right away. I said, "That's easy. It's called a 'for-sale' sign."

When I drove back to Coldfoot and dropped into the valley for the first time since my evacuation, I despised what I saw. My life was more important than the business. Cathy wanted out, anyway. We both were suffering physically. Coldfoot had grown too big for us to handle. But how difficult would it be to unload the place?

Princess had made an offer in 1987. When the bus traffic revved up, Tim McDonnell said Princess was prepared to offer $1 million to buy me out. I wasn't ready to leave then. Besides, Princess had stipulated that if it bought Coldfoot, Cathy and I would have to run the place for another five years. That wouldn't work. As soon as I signed the papers, they would start dictating from Seattle how the place should be run. I asked for $1.5 million so that we would get out with a million after taxes. Princess wouldn't budge, and that was that. Cathy was disappointed. She was ready to go.

In 1989, I called Princess back, and was told, "You had your chance." The company wasn't interested. Neither was Holland America. I let it be known that Coldfoot was for sale, and lowered the price to $1.1 million. I made it clear that the moment the sale was arranged, I would walk out the door—a mistake, I realized later. I should have set myself up as a consultant.

In January 1990 Petro Star Refinery of North Pole, a subsidiary of the Arctic Slope Regional Corporation, put up a $50,000 non-refundable deposit to secure a six-month purchase option. An appraiser from Price Waterhouse in New York spent three days at Coldfoot looking the place over, and recommended in favor of the purchase.

Steve Lewis from Petro Star flew up, and we sat in a corner of the cafe writing out the details on a couple of napkins. I made it clear I had to walk away the day after the papers were signed, and he said that was fine, that if they needed me they shouldn't be buying Coldfoot. We didn't own the land, so they were getting the thirty-year lease with BLM, the liquor license, the wrecker service, and rights to the logo.

We made a deal on July 3, and Cathy and I left Coldfoot. Daughter Kaye was manager in the interim while the new owners assumed control. We were to finalize the paperwork in August, exactly a year after I had become ill. But by then the attorneys had gotten involved and all sorts of tax issues came up. Petro Star made me sign a clause saying if any environmental violations were discovered, the price could be lowered. Of course, they found something and re-negotiated the price down by about $100,000.

As badly as I wanted to get out—I *needed* to get out—I missed Coldfoot something awful. More than a decade later, I still miss it. If I could get a piece of land up there, I might even go back. Who knows? I love the country, but I loved the people even more. Probably ninety percent of the truckers were regulars we saw on a regular basis the entire nine years we were at Coldfoot. They were like family.

Coldfoot was special to me, though. I've gone back to visit half a dozen times, just to see it, or show it off to friend. But I'm not nostalgic. Life goes on.

Once, years before, as I flew over the Brooks Range, I happened to look down into a ravine and saw the faint outline of what appeared to have been a ten-by-ten-foot cabin where two creeks came together. This made me reflect. I saw myself as having been tough living in a tent and an old school bus at Coldfoot in the beginning, but I had an all-weather road to drive on. This lonely, remote place glimpsed from an airplane had been home to somebody who had to pack in everything, and build from scratch. Now *that* guy was tough, a pioneer.

Yet, many years from now, somebody may drive to Coldfoot on a smooth, paved road, look at historic photographs of what I started with and what I built in this cold, faraway place, and he's going to shake his head and think—that Dick Mackey was tough, a pioneer.

The farthest north spruce tree on the Dalton Highway.

On to our next adventure

The mother bear looked up, saw the two women across the stream, and charged across the water in about four steps, then stopped. This was an exciting moment.

We managed to spend some idle time in Hawaii.

THE MOMENT we signed the papers on Coldfoot, Cathy and I were out of there. But the next phase of our life began earlier when I was ill. After the tests in Seattle, the doctors shipped me back to Anchorage for more tests as an outpatient. We stayed at the Mush Inn Motel across the street from a place that sold recreational vehicles.

One day, I said to Cathy, "I'm going stir crazy in this room. Let's go look at those RVs for something to do."

We looked at a little RV called a Class C, and were stunned by the price—$43,000. A veterinarian I knew owned the dealership. I mentioned that Rick was living in the Trapper Creek area, and that we planned to drive the one hundred or so miles up there for the weekend.

He suggested we take the RV to find out if we liked that style of travel. Well, this was like giving candy to a baby. That lousy sneak knew what he was doing—the little model we drove up to see Rick wouldn't be big enough for us. At nine o'clock Monday morning, we returned the RV and on the same day bought the largest RV in the showroom, a thirty-two-foot Class A motor home, for $59,000.

We fell in love with RVs. Two weeks later we took a six-week driving trip along the West Coast. After the Coldfoot deal closed, we put our belongings into storage in Fairbanks and set out in the RV. We didn't have a home anymore. Then, we upgraded to a forty-foot motor home. We were going to enjoy life, and go where the birds went. First, however, we agreed that Kris could go to a public school for her senior year of high school. It was the first time since elementary school that she would be able to attend a real school.

The place we chose to park for that year was Branson, Missouri, the famous hotbed of country and western music. That part of Missouri is in the Ozark Mountains and has small farms, lakes, good fishing, and lots of outdoor activities. What attracted me was an article in the local newspaper. A teenager had stolen a guitar, and the newspaper published his name. The community seemed to be saying, "You'd better behave." We liked that attitude.

We bought a house from a dentist who went bankrupt, fixed it up, and sold it after a year. While we were there, we saw Loretta Lynn, Willie Nelson, Merle Haggard, Ray Stevens, Mel Tillis, and Wayne Newton. Branson is a town of about four thousand residents, but millions of tourists pass through each year.

This was just our temporary home. Kris graduated in May 1992, and the next morning we were on the road again. Sounds like a country song title, doesn't it? We headed back to Alaska, planning to build a permanent home. We didn't want to live in a city, so we drove between Delta and Nenana looking for property. We ended up at Nenana, a couple of miles down the Parks Highway from Rick and his family.

We have the best Alaska has to offer. We're on the highway system. In five minutes I'm in downtown Nenana and in forty-five minutes I'm in Fairbanks. We're in a wooded area. We have good hunting and fishing. We don't have close neighbors as you would in town, but we have neighbors a short distance away. And we've got family north and south of us.

We had help with the basics, but Cathy and I did a lot of the work ourselves putting up a new log home. I can't get away from construction, I guess. I love to build, just not everyday. We lived in the RV for the summer of 1992 before the house was ready. By this time our RV of choice was a full-scale, bus-sized vehicle converted into a luxurious RV.

Once we moved into the house, though, the RV sat there. In the winter of 1993, we drove Outside. We stayed in a fancy RV park in California, where we met people who told us they'd always wanted to go to Alaska. But they were afraid to travel north in their big buses, having heard horror stories about the Alaska Highway.

I said, "Well, look at our RV. It's been up and back, and nothing bad happened."

I began to think there might be a niche market for high-end RV tourism. These people had more money than they knew what to do with and were looking for something new. They wanted to go first class all the way. That was the key. All kinds of guided RV trips to Alaska are available in which you get out at a picnic table and eat a hot dog. But my trip had to be top-of-the-line. Cathy and I spent the next summer on a scouting mission, traveling through Alaska and the Yukon designing a forty-five-day tour.

We put together a 4,000-mile guided trip that began around Memorial Day at Dawson Creek, British Columbia at Mile 0 of the Alaska Highway, and ended back in Prince George, B.C. around the Fourth of July.

We contacted retirement places in Arizona, California, and Florida to drum up business. The only thing the customers had to do was drive their buses and put in their diesel fuel. We chartered planes for side trips to Prudhoe Bay and Barrow. We arranged fishing trips for king salmon and halibut. We charged $8,000 per vehicle, for two people, all-inclusive including gratuities. Sixteen buses signed up the first year, and Cathy and I led the caravan.

Dalton Highway truckers used to call those big buses "stagecoaches," so Cathy came up with a name for our enterprise—Arctic Stagecoach Tours.

We didn't need to advertise because we got so many word of mouth referrals. We escorted caravans in 1994, 1995, and 1996. I enjoyed this new adventure, though Cathy was a little less forgiving than I was of some of the strong personalities who got on her nerves. We were dealing with multi-millionaires and hard-charging businessmen used to getting their way.

In Lakeland, Florida, I had a mural painted on the side of our bus advertising who we were and where we were from. The mural depicted an Iditarod dog team, a wall tent at a hunting camp, and a stagecoach. The stagecoach was a tie to my hometown of Concord, New Hampshire, where Wells Fargo stagecoaches had been made.

At Dawson Creek, we spent two days getting organized. We stayed at an RV park run by a young couple just getting started, and the two of them put on a huge feed for us featuring moose steaks. Our customers loved it. We also visited a museum where everyone learned about the Alaska Highway, built by the military in 1942 as a World War II supply link to Alaska.

Next stop was Fort Nelson. The first night, a banker from Michigan nervously asked if the road was going to get any worse. He had heard stories about how bad the road was, filled with potholes and rocks, and I had been telling them they would be fine. I reassured him.

Well, the highway is paved all the way now, but there are rough patches. The secret is to go slow. These were heavy rigs, weighing more than fifty thousand pounds. Most towed cars. We never exceeded the speed limit and more often than not ran under the speed limits.

Cathy and I were pace setters and had to be careful. In some places it's illegal to run a convoy. We had to leave room for other vehicles to pass. We were all connected by CB radios, and I did a lot of talking. I filled the air with tales from the Iditarod. We always stopped at Iditarod headquarters in Wasilla.

We had fun along the way. We visited hot springs. We took in the gold-rush revues in Whitehorse, Yukon Territory. We took boat rides. And wherever we went, fine dining awaited us. We arranged special meals, and had Arctic Stagecoach Tours menus printed that the customers took home as souvenirs.

I made sure the whole gang got a chance to stay at Coldfoot. Of course, we flew there. No way were we going to drive those buses on the Dalton Highway. In Barrow, we visited the site marking the crash of Will Rogers and Wiley Post, watched Eskimo dancers, and dined at Pepe's—the world's farthest north Mexican restaurant. The owner, Fran Tate, entertained us with local color. Of course, we went to Denali National Park to view wildlife. I have a photograph with seven grizzly bears in it. Near Fairbanks, we visited the Little El Dorado Gold Mine, where we went down into a gold mine, and we cruised on the stern wheel riverboat *Discovery*. We flew into Anaktuvuk Pass, we went to Valdez to see the pipeline, and we made side trips to Seward and Homer.

Homer was a welcome break. We spent four days there. Our people fished for king salmon and halibut, took sightseeing flights, and had time off to relax and do nothing.

The size of Alaska made a big impression. These tourists were stunned that you could drive a hundred miles and see no people. And they appreciated the wilderness. Our customers saw more of Alaska than some Alaskans who have lived in the state for thirty years. I was on the CB all of the time relaying information and telling stories. Cathy accused me of uttering a little too much BS, but I thought of it as salesmanship.

Some strange things happened, too. Once, we stopped at Hyder to observe bears. They were all over the place on Fish Creek. Cathy and I and another couple, Wes and Lorraine, went back for a second viewing in the evening, watching a sow teach her cubs how to fish. When the cubs ran out into the water, the mother pushed them back if they got in too deep. Then she caught the fish and brought it to them. We stood transfixed for about two hours. It was fascinating.

The sow was enormous, and the cubs were good-sized, too, maybe yearlings. We had parked parallel to the stream, and got out to watch. This was not one of the customary viewing areas, and in retrospect this may have not been a smart place to observe bears close at hand. The bears are accustomed to people on the elevated platform and ignore them there.

At any rate, after a while, the sow disappeared. Wes and I climbed back into the Jeep. Cathy smoked a cigarette as she and Lorraine stood at the top of the riverbank. Suddenly, the mama bear poked her head out of the brush next to the stream, directly across from where the women were standing.

You don't want to rile a sow with cubs. The sow looked up, saw the women, and shifted into overdrive. I mean she charged across the water in about four steps. The bear stopped at the bottom of the bank and looked up. Well, this was an exciting moment. Wes was in the driver's seat, and I said quietly, "The thing to do is drive the vehicle between the bear and the women *right now.*"

There was just enough room to do this if the women would backpedal a little. Wes started the engine, and I got the door open. I thought the women would back up slowly. But they made a dash for the Jeep. Wes's door was locked. He said, "Go around." His wife said, "You're crazy," and dove in the window right on top of him.

The bear just stood there, probably laughing. This could have ended badly, but apparently the bear just wanted to scare us away. And she did that. The humorous part was watching Lorraine dive through the window.

We educated these tourists about Alaska. We introduced them to the different cultures. They came to understand that I'm a guy who hunts. I haven't bought meat at a grocery store for forty years. And I drive dogs. My son Bill ran a trap line. One customer said something that I've not forgotten, because it scared me.

He said, "The only reason you can live this lifestyle, the way you exist, is because people of my generation understand it. When we're no longer here, the younger generation will not accept you living like this, differently from the way the rest of the country lives."

Oh, I hope he's wrong.

From tour guide to commentator

I climbed onto an ice floe and jumped off the other side, plunging into the Arctic Ocean over my head. The ice-cold water took my breath away.

Our next adventure was guiding RV tours to Alaska.

WE WERE PARKED next to a lake in British Columbia one spring a day after the ice went out, and ice floes were everywhere. One of our outgoing customers, Kim, was ribbing me about being Mr. Alaska and daring me to jump into the frigid water.

Everybody was standing around the campfires about fifty feet from the water while Kim heckled and teased me. He was fixated on the subject. Then he said, "If you jump in, I'll kiss your butt at high noon in Anchorage and invite the governor to the ceremony."

If he had bet me $50, I would have ignored him, but this offer was interesting. At first I let him go on without responding, then I slipped quietly into the motor home. I put on a pair of old Levis and tennis shoes and then burst out of the RV, running for the water and yelling, "Call the governor" as I leaped into the water.

The water was cold, but I was in it for only a few seconds. Kim was stunned, but he laughed his head off. I had called his bluff, and there wasn't much he could say.

On a side trip to Prudhoe Bay a few weeks later, we were on a tour that took us to the edge of the Arctic Ocean. All of a sudden, Kim blurted out, "I dare you to jump into the Arctic Ocean." Everybody looked at Kim and me. Somebody said, "You must be nuts to make a bet like that after what Dick did a few weeks ago." I said, "No, I'm not going to jump into the Arctic Ocean."

Then, Kim said, "I'll give you a plane ticket to Hawaii and a week's vacation if you'll jump into the Arctic Ocean."

I said, "I don't go if Cathy doesn't go." He laughed and said, "Alright, I'll make it for two."

We all laughed, the subject was dropped, but I got to talking with the tour guide. I said, "Boy, that water has got to be cold." He said, "We have something called the Prudhoe Bay Polar Bear Club. I'm a member and will vouch for you if you go in. You'll get a certificate, too."

He said he club had plenty of blankets and other gear for swimmers in the rear of the bus, and added, "You could do it." I got back onto the bus and took off everything except my Levis. This time I didn't have extra clothing.

Huge hunks of ice floated in the water—a perfect visual aid for this lunatic jump. When the blankets and first aid were ready, I dashed into the ocean, and everybody looked up. The water was surprisingly shallow. To get a Prudhoe Bay Polar Bear Club certificate, I had to immerse myself, but already my legs were stinging from the cold.

The water was only up to my thighs after I walked out a couple of hundred yards, so I climbed up onto an ice floe and jumped off the other side, finally plunging into icy water over my head. The cold took my breath away, and I was shaking uncontrollably by the time I got back to shore.

Frankly, the experience was scary. People later told me I was an idiot to do this. Apparently people have had heart attacks from the shock of the cold water.

When we got to Anchorage, we were having dinner at the Regal Alaskan Hotel when Kim showed up with a plastic bag containing a towel and washcloth. Kim told me that while he had not contacted the governor, he was ready to settle our bet. After dessert, I made a little speech.

I said, "I have a confession to make. You all know what the bet was, but I'm backing out." Everyone looked at me. "No matter how much Kim scrubs his face, I'm not going to let him kiss my butt." He cracked up and so did everybody else. That closed the book with him.

Cathy and I had a lovely week in Hawaii, however.

We conducted bang-up tours those years. Our tour cost twice that of any of the others, yet there was a great demand for what we offered, and we didn't even have to advertise.

In the beginning we thought we might run the tours until Kris was ready to take over. She was studying tourism industry management and public relations at college. But we walked away from it. We didn't need the income, and the enterprise began to consume too much of our time.

I've reached the point where I cringe if I have to follow a schedule. Running the tours put me on a schedule day after day. I hated it when something went wrong. Once in a while it did. We'd get to a campground, and they had forgotten you were coming. We'd show up at a restaurant with thirty people, and they had overlooked your reservation. I might have stuck with the business a while longer, but it didn't take much encouragement from Cathy to persuade me to try something different.

The greatest satisfaction was that we made some great friends. Just about everyone who traveled with us said ours was the best tour they ever experienced anywhere in the world.

You might say that running Arctic Stagecoach Tours was my last real career, but I didn't settle into a rocking chair.

I did Iditarod commentary for Channel 13 in Anchorage for several years during the 1990s. The station wanted someone who knew the mushers to provide color. I shared my experiences, talked about the one-second victory, and did a little analysis. I never predicted a winner, but did identify several mushers capable of winning. I didn't go out on a limb and I didn't stir up any controversy. That wasn't my role.

After a while doing commentary lost some of its luster. At the ceremonial start in Anchorage I sat at a flimsy card table for four hours and then did the same thing the next day at the re-start in Wasilla. No one will ever accuse me of being shy or running out of things to say, but I missed walking up and down Fourth Avenue mingling with the mushers and the dogs. And I wasn't able to watch Rick after he left the starting line. I missed being close to the action.

In 2000, a year after Joe died of cancer at age eighty-two, I watched the race with Vi Redington in front of her home in Knik. Mushers tossed flowers as they passed. One musher saluted. It was a beautiful tribute to Joe.

Advisor, actor, and stunt man

*I was driven to the set of 'White Fang.' I couldn't
even dress myself. A woman fixed my hair and
applied makeup. Cathy and I couldn't stop laughing.*

We had great fun helping film "White Fang" in 1990.

GIVEN HOW MUCH I talk, it seems ironic I didn't end up with a speaking part in the *White Fang*, a Disney movie based on the Jack London novel.

A company that specialized in finding film locations contacted the Iditarod Trail Committee and, in early 1990, I got a call asking would I be interested in providing dogs and being a technical advisor for the movie.

The goal was to make an authentic movie. The director wanted to use old-style harnesses on freight dogs, which are bigger than the slimmed-down

Iditarod racing dogs. The concept was based on historic photographs. My contract called for me to provide ten dogs.

I was supposed to teach the actors how to mush dogs and to maneuver on snowshoes, too. Ethan Hawke was the star. Other actors played trappers. Filming would take place near Haines in Southeast Alaska.

I found a guy in Wiseman to supply dogs and to accompany them to Haines. My daughter Kris was hired to care for the dogs. The movie people rented a house with lots of land about twenty-five miles from town, and we filmed there for six weeks.

It was a new experience. I'm not much of a moviegoer, so I didn't know anyone on the set. After we arrived with the dogs, the director brought three actors out onto the snow where the big shots were going to be filmed. I was supposed to provide instruction on this wide-open frozen swamp.

None of the actors had been on a dog sled, and probably hadn't even seen one. They had trouble staying upright on the back of the sled and trouble holding on. They couldn't walk on snowshoes. Constantly they fell down in the snow and weren't having any fun. But Ethan Hawke and the other actors gobbled up the chocolate-chip cookies that Cathy baked.

The director watched this fiasco for about three days. His group wasn't making much progress, so he decided on a fresh approach. He wanted to know if he could dress me up to resemble each of the characters with a scene on snowshoes or on a dog sled. I said sure, it sounded like fun.

This expanded my involvement in the movie. In one scene, for an instant, you can recognize me if you look quickly. Look for the campfire scene where a wolf has attacked a guy. I'm the prospector who comes in to save him.

In the middle of filming, we had a problem. Apparently Joe from Wiseman could be on the set because the dogs belonged to him. Kris was OK because she was getting one hundred dollars a day to care for the dogs. But Cathy couldn't be there because she wasn't on the payroll. I wasn't happy about that development, so they fixed it by hiring Cathy to cook for Kris and me! That put Cathy on the payroll.

Filming was tedious. We had a lot of retakes, over and over. It took hours to set up scenes with special effects. But it was interesting to see how the whole thing unfolded.

A representative of People for the Ethical Treatment of Animals was on the set to ensure care of the animals. He irritated me. He was so unrealistic. He would say something like, "We can't traumatize this dog." This drove me crazy. You couldn't do this and you couldn't do that. He didn't understand sled dogs at all.

It was all little picky stuff. I showed him that the dogs didn't mind being put in harness, and that they liked settling down by a campfire. He thought I put booties on the dogs' feet to protect them from cold. He about flipped when he found out the booties protected them from running on ice. "They might cut their feet?" he said. "Oh, heavens, we can't allow that!"

If you were going fast, and the dogs shied in the least, he felt you needed to give them R&R for a week. This drove me nuts, but I had to put up with it. As time went on, I worked with the guy, got him to pay attention, and made him understand how dogs behave. He finally got a grasp of it.

Things became more interesting as my role increased. In one scene, two guys are transporting a coffin down a three-hundred-foot embankment. It was a risky situation. They were trying to slow the descent so they don't pick up too much speed and fall through the ice at the bottom. They wanted me to mush along the top of the embankment, then make a right-hand turn, and start down the cliff. But there was no way you could stop the dogs and keep your footing. This is where the coffin falls. It was too realistic.

I told the director I couldn't do it with the dogs. It wouldn't work for me to be in front of them with a loaded sled going down the hill. He told me I could do it, that it all came under the heading of doing stunts. Now I was a stunt man!

The crew manipulated the terrain a little bit to make the scene easier, then attached a harness under my clothing and fastened the other end to the collar of a dog to prevent the team from pulling away. None of us considered the possibility that the dog might pull the collar off of me. Three cameras were spaced around to get the shot because it was going to be a one-time deal.

I was still telling the director it wouldn't work. He said, "Give me two seconds on your feet—that's all I need." I started thinking this scene might be hazardous to my health.

Finally we began filming. I mushed the dogs parallel to the top of the cliff and instantly the coffin flew off the sled. The lead dog spooked and jerked the collar. I went flying all over the place, tumbling down the bank, and the dogs came with me. Nobody got hurt, but it was a true action shot. I must have stayed on my feet for the required two seconds because the director came running over, yelling, "Perfect shot! Just what I wanted!"

During filming of a scene by the campfire, where I appear on camera, things got out of hand. The wolf, a hybrid, runs in and jumps on a guy. They attracted the wolf by placing chunks of raw meat under the actor's clothes and then dousing him with meat juices. The wolf broke through the guy's skin.

The campfires were set with propane and operated with valves. I had speaking lines—part of a conversation about furs—in the scene where the prospector comes to the rescue.

I had made the commercials for Timberland on a Screen Actors Guild exemption. That meant the producers paid a fine because I wasn't in the union. But there is a limit to the exemptions, so this time I had to join the guild. Disney paid my dues. It wasn't until eleven-thirty the night before the scheduled shoot that I was given a contract to sign. It was my fourth contract for *White Fang*.

The next morning, a station wagon pulled up. The driver said, "Mr. Mackey, I'm here to pick you up." On the set, I found a door with a star and my name on it. I couldn't believe it. I couldn't even dress myself. A woman fixed my hair and applied makeup. Cathy and I couldn't stop laughing.

After all that, filming was interrupted after half a day, and everything was put on hold for ten days. I never knew why. I was being paid five hundred dollars a day for this little part. The director later told me I was probably the highest paid person on the set because of all the jobs I had.

Darned if this scene didn't get cut from the finished picture. And I had to audition too! This was really no surprise because nothing in this scene connected with the other scenes. It didn't fit.

We saw the movie several times when it came out, and later I bought a videotape copy. Having been behind the scenes has ruined movies for me. Now I pick them apart. However, when we saw the movie for the first time, Cathy and I were amazed to see how it had come together, especially the special effects.

I get residuals every time *White Fang* shows on TV. They are down to something like $100 a month, but they keep coming. They're in addition to the $75,000 I made for six weeks work. What a deal!

If anyone wants a consultant for *Call of the Wild*, I'm ready.

My character was cut from the final version of the film.

Traveling to faraway events

When we returned to the Trans Italia, the innkeeper kissed me on both cheeks. The guy was so friendly he could hurt you. This was typical Italian hospitality.

One winter I was invited to Norway. That's Russia across the river.

MUSHING CROSSES international boundaries. The only difference from one country to another is saying "Gee" and "Haw" to the dogs in a different language.

The combination of my Iditarod background and the TV commentaries kept my profile high in the dog-mushing world, and that attracted invitations in the early 1990s to serve as race marshal for mushing events in Europe.

The first event was the Trans-Italia. The connection was Italian musher Armen Khatchikian, who competed in the Iditarod in 1984, 1985, and 1986. He received so much attention at home that the president of Italy invited Armen into his home.

Armen became a sports hero. He started a mushing school and wrote an instructional book filled with pictures of Joe Redington. Armen even provided dogs for a movie made in Italy by Sylvester Stallone.

Armen organized a stage race and invited me to be race marshal. The stages took place all over northern Italy, though the total racing distance was less than four hundred miles. After finishing each stage, we drove for many hours to get to the next one. A single stage might be as short as twelve miles, but the distance between stages was hundreds of miles. The place was as much an attraction as the race. We saw so much beautiful country. We started in Cortina d'Ampezzo, site of the 1956 Winter Olympics, and went from there to ski resorts and picturesque mountain villages. Our reception was unforgettable in the small villages.

The Trans-Italia more or less paralleled the French Alpirod, which is more famous and has been run by many Alaskans. The sponsoring Italian communities were smaller and, unlike the Alpirod, this event required mushers to camp out in tents. One memorable stop was on the side of a mountain at a tiny inn run by a man and his wife and daughter. The inn looked down on the home village of Fiorello LaGuardia, once mayor of New York. Roman soldiers built the ancient village two thousand years ago. LaGuardia gave a snow blower to the village to improve winter access to the place. I can't think of a road in Alaska that compares to the road with its miles of switchbacks leading to the village.

I invited the innkeeper to sit next to me at the head table for dinner. I thanked him for the wonderful hospitality, and complimented him on the great food. Through an interpreter, he told me this had given him prominence in the village. When I returned the next year, the innkeeper hugged me and kissed me on both cheeks. This guy was so friendly he could hurt you. This was typical of the treatment we received.

The field usually consisted of about forty mushers, many from Scandinavian countries. There were a few familiar Americans. Including Tim White of Minnesota, the famous sled-builder, and Libby Riddles, the 1985 Iditarod champion. Tim has helped organize more sled-dog races around the world than anyone else. He helps get them started, participates, and then moves on to the next one. He's had a major influence on the sport.

As race marshal, I was concerned with trail management. Often we had to alter the course due to limited snow. We raced stages of fifteen miles at most, but snow was always an issue. For the most part, the dogs weren't as well trained as Alaska dogs, though much of the time the winner would finish a stage in less than an hour.

The socializing seemed to be as important as the competition. Everyone had a good time. Every night there was lots of food and wine, including special wines made by innkeepers along the way.

The media gave the event a lot of attention because mushing was a novelty. At the ski resorts, the lifts could have been shut down during the sled dog races because everybody came to see the dogs. As we got closer to Rome, the crowds grew larger. Tim White won the Trans-Italia the first year, winning $3,000. Libby placed second the year she came.

I almost always had a great time in Europe—except for the time I came home from Kirkenes, Norway suspected of being a spy. I had been invited to represent the West at a mushing event. A musher from central Siberia represented the East. Kirkenes is in the far north of Norway, not far from Murmansk, Russia.

I had agreed to do TV commentary for the Iditarod, so I had to be in Anchorage by the first Saturday in March. That meant the Norway trip would be rushed. I never did find out how I happened to be invited. The sponsors had little for me to do, just be seen and talk to people.

The 250 miles of racing would take place on a river separating Norway and Russia. Across the river from Kirkenes were abandoned Russian guard towers. I borrowed a snowmachine and dashed over there to climb a guard tower and get a picture taken. It was an "I've been to Russia" thing. Nobody shot at me. Nobody arrested me. It was no big deal.

After my whirlwind swing through northern Norway, I headed for Alaska by way of New York. That's where the fun started. A customs official asked where I was coming from. I told him Kirkenes, Norway. He asked to see my tickets and wanted to know the purpose of my visit. I told him I went there for a sled-dog race. He looked at another officer and asked me to "Step this way."

They took me to a little interrogation room and sat me down at a table. A second official came in, then a third, and the questioning continued. Why I was in Norway for only sixty hours? I told them again—a sled-dog race. They looked at one other. Meanwhile, customs had intercepted my luggage, which had been checked through to Anchorage. Thirty minutes we were squeezed into the little room—three customs agents, my luggage, and me.

They wondered why my only contact with the Norwegians had been with somebody in Kirkenes whom I could not identify who bought my airplane ticket. The ticket had been waiting for me in New York. The next question was, "Why would anyone spend $2,000, and pay in cash, for you to fly to Norway for that short length of time?"

Stupidly, I said, "I guess because they like me." That was my way of easing the tension, but the customs people didn't laugh. Instead, they searched my luggage. Then one official asked to see my wallet. She looked through all my cards and came across the one that said, "Lifetime membership, Iditarod Sled Dog Race." She asked how I happened to be a lifetime member, and I told her because I was one of the organizers and had won the race in 1978.

She said, "Do you know that woman who wins the race?" I said, "Susan Butcher?" And she said, "Do you know Susan Butcher? Have you ever met her?" And then it was all over. That's all it took clear the air. Thanks to the Iditarod, they decided I wasn't a spy. The woman ran the two guys out and we sat there for fifteen minutes BSing about the Iditarod!

This hullabaloo occurred because Kirkenes is about twenty minutes from a Murmansk submarine base that was supposed to be secret at the time. The feeling at customs was that if I wasn't dealing in drugs, I must have sneaked into the submarine base. Why I would do that, I don't know.

Before leaving, I gave the customs agent several of my Iditarod cards—the ones that look like baseball cards—as a souvenir. What an experience.

In 1999, I was invited to serve as race marshal for an event run through the Pyrenees in Spain. About fifty mushers took part. The race was good, but some of the accommodations and food were not. Cathy and I came down with something a couple of days after arriving. This turned to pneumonia, and we were taken to a hospital, deathly ill.

However, we weren't allowed to stay in the hospital because we didn't have travelers insurance. We said we would pay with credit cards, but the rules required insurance—period. So we were hurriedly put onto a plane headed back to the United States. When we got to Fairbanks, we went straight to a doctor. When we were invited back to Spain the next year, Cathy and I looked at each other, and said, "No thanks!"

My other work as a race marshal work has been in Alaska—at the Kuskokwim 300 in Bethel and at the Fireplug 150 in Ester—and at the Upper Peninsula 200 in Michigan. I still go to the UP race. I'll keep going back as long as they'll have me.

I have been in situations in Michigan where it was necessary to get involved in disputes because rules were unclear. Once, the trail wasn't marked properly, and it cost a racer the championship. Another time, seven teams got into trouble in water on a two-mile stretch of historic trail, and scratched. How do you deal with a musher who doesn't have all the required gear? Or mushers screaming at one another because one wouldn't allow the other to pass? Sometimes I had to make judgment calls. Most of the time I helped fine-tune the rules for the next race.

Most race rules are well defined. It says, "You may," "You shall," "You must." Or, a specific monetary or time penalty is required. But often, too, there is a clause that says, "the race marshal, in conjunction with..." That means other judges, veterinarians, or members of a board of directors might be brought into a dispute. Usually rulings can be made with latitude. Participants have to believe you are fair.

Some ancient trails in the Alps had been put in by Roman soldiers.

I once made a controversial call to cancel the Fireplug after the start when the temperature dropped to 60 degrees below zero. My reasoning was this: If you cut off training at 40 below due to the cold, why would you want to push your dogs by racing at 60 below? It isn't what the musher wants; it's what's reasonable for the dogs.

Yukon Quest and the Iron Dog

*I was race marshal for the Iron Dog, the world's longest
snowmobile race. Some saw me a traitor to mushing because of
long-standing animosity between mushers and snowmachiners.*

Sons Dick and Rick rest in the 1997 Yukon Quest.

I MAY HATE schedules, and I'm too beat up to race, but I do like to stay
involved in mushing. This may be why I ended up on the board of directors of
the Yukon Quest International Sled Dog Race.

The Quest is a 1,000-mile race between Fairbanks and Whitehorse,
Yukon Territory, which alternates directions each year. It got its start in 1984,
and some people consider it to be the anti-Iditarod, or a throwback to the
original Iditarod. It doesn't get the same media coverage as the Iditarod. It's
not as expensive to run and to train for, but a lot of mushers believe the Quest
is a tougher race than the Iditarod.

The Quest has more hills, fewer checkpoints, and its rules require racers
to run from start to finish with a single sled. You break it, you fix it, or you're
out of the race.

A few years ago son Rick took a hiatus from the Iditarod and moved over to
the Quest. Rick raced three times, placing third, second and first. He won in

1997. My granddaughter Brenda raced in 1998. She's the first of the next genera-tion of Mackeys to become a competitive musher, and this was her debut in a long-distance race.

The people who started the Quest thought the Iditarod had become too commercial. There's a feeling that the Iditarod is an Anchorage race and the Yukon Quest is Fairbanks event. The Quest does have its unique international flavor, although tensions occur between the boards of directors in each country.

I have respect for the Quest, although some mushers perceive it as a training ground for the Iditarod. Rick is the only Iditarod champion ever to go to the Quest, although many other mushers have won the Quest, gone on to the Iditarod, and never gone back. Money is a factor. The Iditarod purse is much richer. In 2001, the Quest winner got $30,000, exactly half of the Iditarod prize for first place. Rick wanted to run the Quest because it was different. It turned out to be good for him.

In the Quest, a trail might be put in by two snowmachines, but it doesn't last and it isn't as smooth as the Iditarod trail. The Quest checkpoints are much farther apart. The hills—mountains, really—are ungodly, especially American Summit and Eagle Summit.

The Yukon Quest people in Fairbanks and Whitehorse have differ-ent and sometimes conflicting perspectives about what the race should be, what type of sponsorships it should have, and other issues. I resigned from the board—several of us did—because we couldn't seem to get beyond these dif-ferences. Maybe we should have gone public to make our case.

I don't mind trying new things. In 1998, I was race marshal for the Iron Dog, the world's longest snowmobile race. Originally it ran one thousand miles and then was stretched to two thousand miles—from the Mat-Su Val-ley to Nome and then to Fairbanks.

Some thought I was a traitor to mushing because of some long-stand-ing animosity between mushers and snowmachiners in Alaska. Resentment has grown among mushers due to snowmachiners tearing up the trail be-tween Big Lake and Nome.

In 1981, I was the Iditarod Race Manager and urged acceptance of Jack Helms, a snowmachine race marshal, to be the Iditarod race marshal. I thought we all should try to get along, and this would be one way to ensure cooperation and mutual understanding. But Jack was not well received. Too much animosity existed, and Jack was perceived as being my yes-man.

We need the snowmachine people. I'm a recreational snowmachiner myself. I've ridden thousands of miles on a snowmachine, putting in trail or training. I don't believe the Iditarod can be run without snowmachines. It's come to a point where mushers expect the trail to be well groomed and packed down by snowmachines.

The idea when we brought in Jack Helms as Iditarod race marshal was that I would reciprocate by becoming a snowmachine race marshal, but it didn't happen for almost two decades.

To follow the Iron Dog, I had to fly. You can't keep up otherwise. They've got superior horsepower. When I'm a race marshal, I make certain at the introductory meeting that everybody knows the rules. I say, "If you don't know a rule, raise your hand." Nobody raises a hand. Then I say, "I'm going to assume that none of you know anything about the rules, and we're going to go over them one by one." Everybody laughs. I promise to enforce the rules fairly. I try to be reasonable and flexible using common sense. But if a situation requires that I come down hard on somebody, I do it.

In the Iron Dog, racers travel in teams of two snowmachines and two drivers. One of the racers used a great deal of profanity, cussing out a teenage volunteer, in Nenana one year. I fined him and made him write out an apology.

It's easier to be race marshal in a snowmachine race than in a dog race. You're working with machinery. The rules are straightforward about what part you are allowed to replace and whether you're on the clock or off. In a sled dog race, you have the additional worry about the health of the dogs. They're flesh and blood. The snowmobiles are metal machines.

Being a race marshal is usually fun. When I consider whether to accept an invitation, I picture a scale with one side being "work" and the other side "fun." The fun side always carries more weight.

It would be exciting to hold a major stage race in Alaska, something like the Alpirod in France or the International Rocky Mountain Stage Stop Race in Wyoming. These are popular events. They aren't as hard on the body as the Iditarod or Quest. And they offer more spectator opportunities by limiting daily runs to forty miles or so.

Rick Swenson and others have pushed for an Alaska stage race, possibly between Wasilla and Fairbanks along the Parks Highway. I don't know whether enough sponsorship money is available to support another race. It's reached the point that if a race doesn't offer a large purse—at least $50,000—mushers aren't interested in competing.

Iditarod mushers who compete in stage races come home to Alaska raving about them. They see these events as a perfect way to train for the Iditarod. If I were a top Iditarod competitor, I would enter the Rocky Mountain race. My dogs would have an easy time of it because of the rest time built into the schedule. I wouldn't be jeopardizing the team's fitness for the marathon races back home.

Who knows? Maybe Alaska will have a big stage race one of these days. Dick Mackey could be race marshal. I guarantee you he would have fun.

Most Alaskans have a bear story

A few feet away a black bear stood on the deck. I ran for the gun cabinet, heart pumping madly. Oh, did I mention that we had left the door open?

The dogs ate well the next winter.

NENANA is a great place to live. Our neighbors are close enough to be neighbors yet far enough away so we forget we have neighbors.

Except for the bears.

Sometimes the bears are the friendliest neighbors of all, maybe *too* friendly. They come over at all hours of the day or night and don't call ahead. They have no manners at all. One "neighbor" was so troublesome that I had to shoot him.

Nenana is a town of several hundred people on the Parks Highway about sixty miles south of Fairbanks. In the fall of 1998, the community closed its dump. Like many Alaska dumps, this one attracted bears who foraged for food among the garbage. So, when the dump closed, the area was left with a bunch of hungry bears with no place to go and—worse yet—no fear of humans.

The area where Cathy and I live is a bear crossing. The black bears and grizzlies don't linger for long, but they pass through often.

One day, we returned from a trip to Fairbanks to find the outdoor barbecue grill had been tipped over on our deck. Something had trampled Cathy's flowerbed, too. She didn't appreciate that. We found bear slobber on the windows and around the door. A bear had tried to get inside.

I took Cathy's 30-06 rifle out of the gun cabinet and loaded it, just in case the bear came back. This was a routine precaution. Bears rarely come up to the house. Our dogs scare them away. Every once in a while, a neighbor will alert us if a bear loiters in the area, mainly to warn people to watch their kids. We get these calls maybe four or five times a summer. The warnings don't alarm you as much as they make you *aware*. This particular night, we got to bed around midnight, and the next thing I know Cathy is hollering, "That bear's back!"

She was awakened by the sound of the grill being knocked over again. One of our dogs came upstairs with its hair standing up on end. I was groggy at first, but went downstairs to investigate. There was a black bear standing right up against the screen door!

I was within three feet of him. I ran for the gun cabinet, my heart pumping madly. Oh, did I mention that we had left the main door open to cool the house? When the bear saw me, it slid down the door and fell through the screen. I worked madly to get the gun cabinet unlocked, but the commotion made me look around for an instant. The bear's head and front paws were inside the house.

I grabbed the gun and shoved a shell in the chamber. The bear backed out and stood up on the deck, peering in at me. Then he dropped down to all fours. Was he going to lunge through the damaged screen door?

I moved forward to within six feet of the door and raised the rifle. BOOM! I fired. The sound inside the house was deafening. I put another round in the chamber. When the first round hit him, the bear must have tightened up all of his muscles. All four claws dug into the wooden deck, and the deep scratch marks can be seen to this day.

Then the bear whirled, dove off the deck, retreated about fifty feet to the garage, and collapsed. I walked over and put another shot into him. I remember this moment vividly. The dusk-like midnight light illuminated the scene, and horrendous mosquitoes swarmed in the muggy air.

Later, I told a newspaper reporter, "It isn't every day you stand in your living room in your skivvies and shoot a bear coming through the screen door."

One of our fall hunting camps.

Under Alaska law, you can kill a bear in defense of life and property, and clearly I was defending both. The bear was big. Stretched out, it filled the eight-foot bed of my pickup truck. I wanted the teeth and claws, but not the hide, as this was an old dump bear and its hide was terrible. Fish and Game said if I shot the bear under the life-and-property defense, the state would get to keep the whole thing, and I would have to fill out a ton of paperwork. But if the bear was shot legally in accordance with hunting regulations, I could keep what I wanted. This was an easy choice. As a senior citizen, I have a permanent hunting license. So, let's call this a midnight bear hunt. I did have to bring in the hide and skull for tagging, though.

I've been a hunter since childhood. I shot my first whitetail deer in New Hampshire at a young age.

We always have meat in the freezer. When I came to Alaska, I had to wait a year to get a resident hunting license. But I went out and got my moose anyway, without a license. We've been eating moose and caribou ever since. That's what the wildlife is there for. If you're a homesteader trying to feed your family, and if you respect the animals and don't waste the meat, you should be able to take what you need.

I try to obey the law. This wasn't always so. When I was younger, living in Wasilla, I poached a moose for meat and got caught red-handed. The local Fish and Game guy saw me, and said, "Oh, Dick. Haven't you got a rifle that isn't as nice as this one that I can confiscate?" I had to turn in the moose, but Fish and Game gave me the next road kill. We needed the meat.

I went on an amazing hunt in the mid-1960s. There was a brief cow moose season in Portage. Four of us parked by the railroad tracks and walked down the right of way. We hadn't gone half a mile when a moose crossed the tracks right in front of us.

The other three guys fanned out into the brush. I decided to continue down the tracks, and this turned out to be a good decision. Blam! I shot a moose. There was another one. Blam! And another. Blam! I shot another moose, and another. It was like a shooting gallery. The moose were criss-crossing everywhere and going down as quickly as I could hit them. Hearing the gunfire, the other guys caught up to me.

The hunt was over in less than an hour. I had done all the shooting. The others had mixed feelings about this. Suddenly I realized I had shot five moose, and there were only four of us. What were we going to do?

We got four moose out of there, gutted the fifth one, and left it in the brush, hoping nobody would find it right away. Back in Anchorage, I asked a friend if he had a harvest ticket for a cow moose. He did. I said, "Well, come on, I've got you one." We drove back to Portage. My friend had a broken arm. So, I had to do all the work. This time, I took a five-dog team and—stupid me—I tossed a piece of meat to the dogs while I skinned the moose and slipped on the icy ground in my mukluks. Boy, then the fight was on.

I grabbed my gun to use as a club to break them up, but I lost my footing and slid right into the middle of the dogfight. I might have been hurt very badly.

I've never been a trophy hunter, only a meat hunter, and I believe strongly that you never waste an animal. My friend sat in the truck the whole time, prepared to tell Fish and Game that he had shot the moose, but couldn't haul it out because of the cast. But nobody came by to ask.

Cathy on a moose hunt.

After the hunt, we packed out moose and black bear meat.

Dogs as a way of life

Men and women follow their dreams to Alaska, fulfill the adventures of their lives, and return triumphant to East Overshoes or wherever. They've run the Last Great Race.

Granddaughter Brenda in the Yukon Quest, 1998.

WOULDN'T IT BE TERRIFIC if seven Mackeys ran the Iditarod in the same year?

A few years back at Christmas, we had a family discussion about that idea— six kids and me, all at once? At my age, the appeal of getting all of us together in the Iditarod is about the only thing that *might* get me back into the race.

Dogs are a way of life. Raising and running them is like being part of 4-H, and it beats hanging out at the pool hall. They are the glue that holds a family together.

My kids were brought up around the dogs. Rick, Bill, and Becky got their starts in the sprint races when they were little. Lance, who is thirty, entered his first Iditarod in 2001. His brother Jason, two years younger, has plans to run. And Kris has a dog background, too, though she hasn't raced in years.

In the winter of 2000-01, more than two hundred dogs were spread around the children and grandchildren. Though I do not express this as often as I should, I'm proud of all the kids, and I like the fact that most of them have dogs. They're keeping alive what I started when I came to Alaska more than forty years ago.

Brenda, Rick's daughter, is the oldest grandchild involved in mushing. She was only eighteen when she raced the Yukon Quest. Brenda doesn't have time for long-distance racing right now. She's a student at the University of Alaska Fairbanks and spends most of her time in Fairbanks. She comes home to help Rick with the dogs and misses this when she's away. Ever since she was a kid she wanted to be a veterinarian. Whatever she does, I know she will be successful.

Would I jump into the Iditarod once more with the kids? Boy, I don't know. When I'm thinking straight I realized my body is too beat up to race the Iditarod any more. Accidents I've had in the construction world have caught up to me. Maybe I could overcome this, maybe not, but I just don't have the dedication it takes anymore. I don't want to be a sightseer. I'm not going to run unless I'm competitive.

So you move on.

I enjoy being involved in mushing as a race marshal, or helping organize a race, without actually running dogs. If I drove down the street to Rick's house and said, "How about me driving a team of your young dogs to Nome this year?" he would be tickled. I might not be competitive, but running would help Rick train those dogs for future races. He's hinted at this, it's an intriguing idea, but I don't see it happening. That first night on the trail I'd be looking for someone to take care of the dogs while I looked for a warm bed for myself.

In 1997, I was handling dogs for Rick in a middle-distance race when a gal approached me and asked if she could take some pictures. Sure, why not? When she had taken two rolls, I laughed and told her she was wasting her film. Little did I know the secret behind those pictures.

Later, when I returned from a trip outside, a box awaited me with a letter and a plaque. I had been named part of the charter class of the Iditarod Hall of Fame for my contributions to the Iditarod and to mushing overall. I thought, "Well, I'll be damned."

Sometimes I contemplate how far the Iditarod has come since the early days working with Joe Redington and watching the race struggle. There have been so many changes since my photo finish. The race once took three weeks to finish. Now it's over in nine days. The only similarity between then and now is that there's a musher behind a sled and dogs in front of it.

To be a contender, training for the Iditarod has to be your life. You have to live and breathe dogs 365 days a year. Mushers are not compensated adequately for what they put into it no matter how large the Iditarod purse.

One of the unique things about the Iditarod is that it's still a great adventure that can be experienced by almost anyone. The ordinary guy sitting behind his desk can chuck his nine-to-five job, train dogs, and enter the Iditarod. Nobody says it will be easy, but it can be done.

These men and women follow their dreams to Alaska, live the adventure of their lives, and return triumphant to East Overshoes or wherever they came from. They're run the Last Great Race.

I admire everyone who has won the Iditarod, especially those who have won it several times and remained hungry to compete again. This requires a special strength. You are never an ex-Iditarod champion. You are a champion—period.

I've had a great life in Alaska, but I have to say that one second at the finish line in the 1978 Iditarod race was perhaps the most important second of my life.

Goldie's kids—49 pups in six litters.

Mackey Family Photos

From top: My parents, Eno and Shirley Mackey, looked on as I received the God and Country Award from the Boy Scouts in 1948; Joan and I with Rick, who was two months old in 1953.

Clockwise from lower left: Son Bill at the start of the 1984 Iditarod; Son Rick at the award ceremony after winning the first Coldfoot Classic in 1984; Granddaughter Brenda at the finish of the Yukon Quest in 1998; Daughter Becky at the 300-Mile Copper Basin Race.

Clockwise from top: Sons Lance and Jason, their mom Kathie, and me at Jason's wedding in 1992; Lance just after crossing the finish in the 2001 Iditarod; Jason at the start of the Coldfoot Classic.

Clockwise from top: My grandson Roland Richard, Rick's youngest, is named after the famous sprint musher Roland Lombard; Cathy and me on Father's Day, 1990; Cathy and me with daughter Kristin and grand daughter Angie at the top of Chilkoot Pass in 1990.

From top: Youngest daughter Kristin in front of our Nenana home; Getting ready for hunting season.

INDEX

ABOUT THE AUTHOR

Lew Freedman is the author of 17 books about Alaska, where he lived for seventeen years with his wife Donna and his daughter Abby. A long-time sports editor for the *Anchorage Daily News,* Freedman regularly covered the Iditarod Trail Sled Dog Race.

During the years he wrote about the Iditarod race, Freedman developed a friendship with Dick Mackey and got to know his son Rick, the 1983 Iditarod champion and other members of the family. All the Mackeys kept telling Dick he had to put his stories into book form. When Freedman suggested it, Mackey finally agreed.

Freedman is a gradute of Boston University, owns a masters degree from Alaska Pacific University, and earned a Gannett Foundation fellowship at Colorado State University.

A career journalist, Freedman has served on the staff of the *Philadelphia Inquirer, Florida Times-Union*, and is currently the outdoors writer on the sports staff of the *Chigago Tribune.* Whenever he climbs onto a dog sled he either tips it over or freezes his toes. But one day he says he will run the Iditarod if someone else leads the way and does all the cooking.

Recommendations for readers who want a better understanding of Alaska and its people

ARCTIC BUSH PILOT: A Memoir, by James "Andy" Anderson
as told to Jim Rearden, trade paperback, $16.95

ART & ESKIMO POWER: The Life & Times of Alaskan Howard Rock,
by Lael Morgan, trade paperback, $16.95

COLD RIVER SPIRITS: The Legacy of an Athabascan Irish Family from
Alaska's Yukon River, by Jan Harper-Haines, hardbound, $19.95

COLD STARRY NIGHT: An Alaska Memoir, by Claire Fejes,
trade paperback, $19.95

FASHION MEANS YOUR FUR HAT IS DEAD: A Guide to Good Manners
& Social Survival in Alaska, by Mike Doogan, trade paperback, $14.95

FATHER OF THE IDITAROD: The Joe Redington Story,
by Lew Freedman, trade paperback, $16.95

JIM REARDEN'S ALASKA: Fifty Years of Frontier Adventure,
by Jim Rearden, trade paperback, $17.95

MOMENTS RIGHTLY PLACED: An Aleutian Memoir,
by Ray Hudson, trade paperback, $14.95

OUR ALASKA: Personal Stories about Life in Alaska,
edited by Mike Doogan, trade paperback, $14.95

RIDING THE WILD SIDE OF DENALI, by Miki & Julie Collins,
trade paperback, $14.95

TALES OF ALASKA'S BUSH RAT GOVERNOR: The Extraordinary
Autobiography of Jay Hammond, Wilderness Guide and Reluctant
Politician, trade paperback, $17.95

These and many more Epicenter Press titles can be found at or special-ordered from your local bookstore. Epicenter books also may be ordered from the publisher's website, EpicenterPress.com or by calling 800-950-6663. Prices do not include shipping.

EPICENTER PRESS / Alaska Book Adventures